Manus G. M

Project Failure:

Why Humans can't do projects, (and what to do about it).

A short guide to better managing projects and so reduce project failure. For experienced professionals looking for new perspectives or those relatively new to a project role looking for a fast start to understanding the real world of projects. Also for the nervous and inexperienced stakeholder with responsibility recently thrust upon them.

This book is dedicated to all those brilliant people I've worked with in my career, who were mostly too modest to realise it.

It is also dedicated to those *not* so brilliant people who were usually too immodest to realise it, because at least they provided me with much of the content of this book.

2 nd. Edition
June 2020.

PREFACE

If you are involved with projects, as a team member, a sponsor, or simply as an innocent bystander, you must be concerned at the very high failure rate. Despite a wealth of training, methodologies and guidance, projects continue to fail at an appalling rate.

This book looks at the human behavioural, rather than the coldly mechanical, reasons why these failures happen. It suggests some ways to identify if they are happening on your project and proposes some possible solutions.

Luckily, when all else has failed, there is always "Project Bingo"! This provides the team with a way to flag up issues that they see, without the career jeopardy or embarrassment of having to call them out publicly. This will also provide valuable feedback to all levels of management.

CONTENTS

INTRODUCTION.

The track record of IT projects is a bit of a horror show with recent research estimating that less than 40% of projects actually deliver on their proposed benefits. There is no sign that this is likely to improve any time soon. So, is this what is needed – yet another book on how to *do* projects? As the evidence seems to indicate that they don't have much effect, maybe not? Perhaps what is really needed is something which looks at projects from a different perspective? As the title indicates, this book does just that.

This isn't one of those hundreds of conventional manuals which claim to provide a step by step guide, guaranteeing the successful delivery of your project. There probably *are* enough of those already. Instead, this book provides an insight into many of the *actual* reasons why projects fail. This isn't a technical manual on project management, nor is it an academic psychology textbook on human behaviour. Instead, it is an experience based guide to identifying and handling many of the everyday problems that actually cause so many projects to fail.

Throughout this book it refers mainly to IT projects but the lessons are applicable to other types of project, or indeed, many other forms of all too human endeavour.

When humans started building things, at first they weren't very good. In time, with practice, and through sharing what worked, they got better. Eventually, they *almost* never fell down. The same should be true by now of IT projects. Humans have done enough of these, for long enough, for them to rarely fail. Yet they do – to a worryingly high degree. There is a huge industry around training Project Managers, providing appropriate methodologies, tools, techniques, guidance etc, and yet still projects continue to fail. Why is this?

There is a mass of literature on this subject. However, the vast majority of it concentrates on the technical or mechanical aspects. This could be on the methodology, or on some aspect of the technology, or on specific artefacts such as plans. This is understandable, as these things are necessary and can most easily be researched and measured – and hopefully, managed better in the future.

There is also much accumulated and well documented knowledge on how to apply these properly - what are the potential pit-falls, what experience other similar projects have had etc. Yet so many still fail. So, why do humans not learn the lessons, follow the methodology, produce and adhere to good plans etc., – and therefore succeed ?

A key factor is that projects are a *team* sport. It is the failure to really understand and appreciate the consequences of this, that is at the core of so many failures. Currently the focus is almost exclusively on the mechanics of projects and not nearly enough on the human aspects – on how the **team of people,** delivering the project, actually behave. Projects are about a whole bunch of often very diverse people getting together to deliver common objectives. Yet very little attention is given to the consequences of putting people from all around an organisation, or different organisations, together. This is especially concerning given that many of these people will have very little experience of working with others outside of their immediate circle. For example, and without wanting to needlessly reinforce any negative, and completely untrue stereotypes, but most IT staff are not known for their exceptional interpersonal skills.

Projects often start badly. Well intentioned project managers will organize some kind of 'team building' exercise. This will occur at, or near, the beginning - or at least as soon as enough people can be dragged together to form a reasonable approximation of the team. At best, these can be quite useful exercises in being able to put a name to a face or to establish some shared ways of working.

Too often however, these are 'tick box' exercises which are only done because it is the conventional thing to do. They often only increase cynicism – especially amongst those who have experienced many exercises of this type in the past. For this reason, corporate team building exercises rightly make many people shudder. There is very often little else done, or thought given, to deal with the mass of complex, inter-personal relationships and personal agenda's which are, in fact, a major project dependency

There are countless project reviews performed every year. It is rare however for the 'softer' or non-mechanical aspects of a project to be analysed to any significant degree. Why is this? Partly this is simply because the importance isn't widely recognised. Mainly however, it is because neither time nor inclination allows anything but the relatively safe mechanical or process aspects of a project to be assessed.

To properly explore the human aspects of a project – such as personal ego issues, or poor interpersonal relationships, or company politics, is too complex – and often politically dangerous. There is, effectively, an unspoken conspiracy to leave it alone; to not go there. If thought about at all, it is perceived as an area where the reviewer just doesn't want to tread.

It is also the case that the reviewers are often simply not qualified to carry out a review in these areas. Yet, as anyone with project experience knows, there is far more to a project than just the mechanics.

So, the purpose of this book is to redress the balance of focus on projects, to emphasise more their essential human aspects. It is not intended that this book replaces the conventional manual, but rather, supplements it. This involves looking at some of the less attractive aspects of human nature such as – playing the 'Superhero', or 'Dog with a bone' syndrome, or 'Conspiracy of Silence'.

The hard part is - how *do* you identify bad practice in team working and allow the necessary issues to be raised in relative safety ? Interpersonal issues are more difficult for most people to deal with because they rarely have the training or coaching to enable them to manage them in a complex work environment. What is needed is a way for people to at least surface issues and in a way which doesn't make them feel vulnerable. It is also important not to make the situation even worse by causing conflict, or embarrassing, or demotivating staff.

The answer is – "*Project Bingo"* ! With "seriousness of purpose and levity of manner", this allows people to highlight these types of problem on a project without personally having to stand up and try and articulate them. It is too often the case that doing this would put their relationship with colleagues, or even their career, at risk. Apart from a valuable source of information for direct line management, Project Bingo improves communication by providing a shared vocabulary for the team on issues. It is also a means of giving feedback on the views of the project team to all who might need it - such as the broader project governance.

How this works is explained in more detail in a later section, but put simply, the book is in 3 main sections. Each of these has a number of components which are the various human behaviours responsible for, or likely contributors to, project failure. It is not intended that each component is covered exhaustively – some of these would require a book on their own. They are, however, covered in enough detail to be able to identify the issue. Each of these components has 3 parts –

- **What is the issue ?** A description of the component.

- **Things to look for**. Help in identifying if this particular problem exists on your project.

- **What to do about it**. Some suggestions on how to deal with it. In many cases, the individual will not be able to do much, but just raising the issue on the bingo card will at least flag up the problem for wider governance.

There is also smaller section which describes how to use 'Project Bingo'. Simply, the components of the 3 main sections are the different elements of the 'Bingo' card. Unfortunately, the more of these that you can tick for your project, the more likely the project is to fail! It doesn't sound like much of a prize, but actually, it could be very valuable for your career.

Finally, as mentioned, this book is not intended as a replacement for the weighty project management manuals which fill the shelves of so many offices. Rather, it is intended to complement these by focusing on aspects that these manuals typically don't cover.

The book is intended to be readable and fairly brief – not because this is not a serious subject, but because project staff almost certainly have enough pressures on their time without unnecessarily adding to it. The idea is for it to be something you can easily dip into occasionally to clarify something or if you think you have identified an issue. It is something for your 'back pocket', rather than to be sat upon a dusty shelf.

MANAGEMENT ISSUES.

This section is concerned with some wide ranging issues on general management activities.

1. POOR DECISION MAKING.

What is the issue ?

One of the differences between a project, and work of an operational nature, is that the number of decisions that need to be taken every day on even a medium sized project is huge in comparison. No one gets them all right, but it is obviously important to get as few wrong as possible – and none of the big ones. Yet so many bad decisions get made on projects. This tends to be because they are made on political or personal grounds i.e. not made with the delivery or technical needs of the project uppermost. Decisions instead are made with no analysis of the facts or any sort of evidence base.

Often, different variations of 'gut feel' or 'instinct' is used in the mistaken belief that this is actually some sort of experience based approach. This may be fine for selecting lottery numbers or choosing which horse to bet on (though it's doubtful) but it isn't the best way to manage a complex IT project.

A slightly more rational basis (though only just) is when people rely on 'whatever worked before'. Unfortunately, this approach tends to be taken without the necessary analysis to determine if the previous experience is actually still relevant or not. Particularly in the complex and fast changing world of IT, this is a very poor basis for decision making.

Bad decisions can also be driven by fear of the new – the apparent right answer looks too new or different from what the decision maker is used to. So the decision is made not on facts or evidence, but from fear of the unfamiliar. It is strange but true that IT people can be every bit as change averse and Luddite as everyone else. This shying away from the new can also be driven by simple laziness – wanting to avoid the hard work that working through a proper process and learning something new, often involves.

Sometimes also, bad decisions come from the fact that the decision maker hasn't got the confidence in their own ability to work through a proper process. They feel they don't know how to go about replacing the current solution, if for example, they have never done a product selection exercise before. Instead, they perform a very superficial decision making process, then play 'safe' with the old, often inappropriate solution. As a result, it often turns out to be anything but the safe option.

Things to look for.

For important decisions there are perhaps two

most obvious signs that a proper decision making process isn't being followed. The first is that a process is followed but it is gone through very superficially. Examples of that would be if there was no real evidence gathering, doing of research, or taking of references. Rather, the conclusion is reached very quickly.

The second is when the decision is being made on personal or political grounds. This would be especially evident if the conclusion reached was one which you might have predicted in the first place e.g. when it is known that certain suppliers or products are preferred.

For the multitude of smaller decisions, when there isn't a formal process to be gone through, the signs of poor decision making are things like -

- A complete lack of consultation.
- Consultation only within the same small clique, rather than with recognised experts in the particular area.
- Decisions which are clearly of a personal nature e.g. who gets what assignment.

What to do about it ?

Decisions should be made in an ego free environment and based on fact or evidence, not emotion or politics. It is up to the leaders on the project to set this standard and impose it. While it would be impractical for all decisions to be formally documented, the significant ones should be and have a clear rationale. This must be documented in a reasonably formal and accessible way e.g. as part of routine progress reporting. Decision makers would therefore be forced to articulate the basis for their decisions and potentially face challenge if necessary.

This approach would set the pattern within the project for all decision making. Not every decision should be challenged, that would be impractical and could lead to the project grinding to a halt, or alternatively, resulting in chaos. However, if decision makers know that the standard is for evidence based, and transparent, decision making, they are less likely to make them in any other way.

Put a tick in the 'Poor Decisions' box.

2. ESTIMATES and BUDGETS.

What is the issue ?.

This is also an area which is very much more a problem for the Waterfall methodology. As discussed previously, when the methodology is focused on scope then the definition of what this actually is, becomes all important. Then, as the estimate in turn is based on this definition, this becomes equally important and problematic.

There are numerous methods for trying to come up with an accurate estimate, from 'Analogy' (i.e. a not very sophisticated way of saying – same as last time), to more 'scientific' methods such as Function Point Counting. Generally, the method is less important than the seriousness and bias-free way with which estimating is approached. For example, keeping some sort of record of what things have taken in the past, with some form of documentation of what was *actually* done.

Another issue is that, however estimating is handled, there will be few people on the project who really understand how it works. Most of the non-IT people on the project will not understand, for example, that estimates are expected to change as requirements become progressively clearer. People are used to getting a quotation to have work done, such as getting their washing machine fixed, or their car serviced, that doesn't change. They expect the same from IT projects. This is an unfair comparison of course. A better one would be with construction projects – which have an even worse record on estimating, if that is possible. Because people don't understand how estimating works, the constant re-estimating or the concept of a Minimum Viable Product is alien to them. A lack of understanding by stakeholders makes managing a key element of the project very difficult.

The estimate itself goes wrong most often when one of two things happens. Either an estimate is based on poor understanding of what is actually needed e.g. at the very start of the project before very much is really known. This is particularly true if it is a very new system. Secondly, if other, 'human' factors are involved which distort the estimate.

For the first of these the Agile methodology copes much better because it is not so Scope focussed. Waterfall tries to fix the problem by attempting to only accurately estimate for the phase for which the most is known i.e. the next one. Too often however, as the project progresses and the requirements become clearer, the project is still expected to stick to the original estimate. This is because the budget has been set and people don't expect, or want, it to change. However, project estimates almost never go down, only up. Some of this is due to a simple lack of thoroughness to include everything that needs to be done. This would be less likely if estimating was given the seriousness and focus it requires. However, even if it is, there will always be the "unknown unknowns" which couldn't have been estimated for at the beginning. Some increase is therefore almost inevitable.

The worst problems occur when the estimates are distorted by 'human' factors. The most common of these are the strong desire by people to do the project whatever the cost, and to increase the scope and importance of their project. In the first scenario there is a fear that the project won't go ahead because the business case won't be positive enough if the costs are too high. So the initial estimates are deliberately kept low.

This happens particularly when things like a new technology is being proposed. The technical people who really want to introduce the technology have a tendency to minimise the costs in order to ensure that it is included in scope. As they are unlikely to be the ones to have to explain to the Very Senior People why the budget has been exceeded, they can be quite relaxed about this.

However, Project Managers can also underestimate in order to have a bigger project which will be higher status in the organization or which will look good on their cv. They calculate that a project which is great experience but which is over budget is better than no project at all.

Of course, the opposite can happen as well – too high an estimate can be produced. While most organizations would prefer a project that finishes under budget to one that goes over, it is still a waste of company resources. This is both because an over generous budget will tend to be spent inefficiently and because the project unnecessarily ties up funding that could be better spent elsewhere.

Even if the organization is pleased that the project finishes under budget it still re-enforces the notion that IT can't estimate properly and will query future estimates – usually looking to reduce them.

Things to look for.

If there appears to be more than the usual keenness to do a project, then the estimates should be suspected of being <u>too low</u>. The over enthusiasm could be generated by a number of different things such as –

- New technology – people are keen to get something new and cool on their c.v.
- High kudos – the project is very high profile and is likely to lead to advancement if it is successful. Even if not successful it will still look good on a c.v. and a prospective new employer won't know about the budget issues.
- A scarcity of project work – if there aren't many other projects to do and there is a fear of having to work on something a lot
- less interesting or even result in redundancy.

If the estimates are being produced by people who don't really have the experience – because it is a new type of system or new technology, then they are unlikely to produce good estimates. There will be a real risk of significant items missed off the estimates – the unknowns.

Over estimates can also happen for a number of reasons, these include –

- People don't want to do the project because it is seen as boring or having very little kudos attached to it. Very high
- estimates are produced in the hope that that will kill the project.
- The project is a must-do for legal or vital strategic reasons. In this case very high estimates are produced because however high, the organization will find the money.
- Also because if the project is that important massive additional contingency is added.
- The project is seen as high risk because of newness of the technology or a perception that it is leading edge in some way, or immature, or just difficult to work with.
- Sometime the estimates are too high simply because the person doing the estimating is too inexperienced. They calculate that it is safer to produce too high an estimate rather than be too low.
- Estimates in specific areas can be inflated by the owner of that area. For example, areas such as Testing or Analysis can be inflated to maximise their importance.

What to do about it ?

If you are convinced that there are grounds for believing that the estimates may be very poor quality – either high or low, there are things which can be done.

Obviously spotting the problem before any budgets are set in concrete is ideal but not always possible. However, the problem should be addressed as soon as possible. The sooner a discussion about the estimates is initiated the better, as leaving it until there is a major budget crisis will only create more bad feeling and make things more difficult to resolve.

The first thing to do is discuss the basis for the estimates. How valid is the suspicion of deliberately bad estimates ? If people have distorted the estimates for their own purposes it will usually be fairly obvious because they won't have a very solid evidence base for them. If possible, finding out about other projects of a similar type will help. This can be done by talking to the supplier for example or another organization which has done a comparable project.

Estimates are more likely to have been distorted if they have been produced by a very small team or even an individual. Another option is to extend the size of the estimating team with the justification of increasing the expertise as much as possible. Any obvious distortions can be rectified by the larger team without blatantly embarrassing the original estimator.

Whether the mis-estimate is high or low, it is important to initiate a conversation within the wider project group. This is so that they understand the estimating process better and any adjustments can be made with as little rancour as possible.

Put a tick in the 'Bad Estimates' box.

3. RESOURCES.

What is the issue ?

In this section it is the people on a project , the human resources, that is the issue rather than other resources such as hardware or software. Even in the rare circumstance when budget isn't a constraint, getting hold of the right number and type of people, when you want them, is still usually a problem. How people go about filling the roles on a project can further compound this. Simplistically, project roles can be filled from either existing, internal resources or from the different types of external resources.

One of the problems with using internal resources is that humans tend to begin by selecting their friends. Good communication and team working are essential so this might sound like a good idea. These things would obviously be more likely to be achieved if people you already know and work well with are in the team. Unfortunately, if the friends are wrong for the roles - because they haven't got the right experience or have the wrong skill set, then this might be a problem. However, if it is only one or two people who are selected in this way, as part of a much larger team, and are given training etc., it should not to be too much of a problem.

If the same type of approach is used but on a larger scale i.e. an existing team is selected whether it has the right experience or not, the problem is going to be very much worse. This can happen because they

are a team that is 'owned' by a very senior manager who has the responsibility to put the project team together and they
want to use their people. Or, it could be a team that has been successful recently on another, but different, project. In the latter example the danger is that the successful team will march, full of confidence and enthusiasm, onto the new project - only to very quickly hit a brick wall due to their lack of appropriate expertise. Thus destroying what could have been great team. Again, while re-using an existing team might apparently solve the team working and comms issues, the lack of expertise will be a more insurmountable problem.

Whether it is a relatively small number of people or a whole team being selected in this way, this is also bad practice because of the impact this will have on the rest of the organization. This will be seen as a powerful clique being selfish with the best work. Others, perhaps better qualified, will be upset at missing out. If appointments are not seen to be being made on merit, all kinds of bad behaviours will quickly develop. Not least of these will be a culture of favouritism, which soon leads to mediocrity – at best.

If there aren't enough resources in-house then, assuming budget is available, the other option is to recruit externally – either permanent or temporary resource.

The issue with recruiting permanent staff is having the expertise to do so if the project is doing something very new. Assuming that the intention is to recruit the skills that the organization is currently lacking, how do the recruiters know what to look for ? How do they know what questions to ask and what does a good answer look like ? Unfortunately, too often recruiters rely on a combination of their own inappropriate expertise and gut feel. This rarely ends well.

Recruiting temporary staff comes in two broad categories. Recruiting a set of individual contractors or going to one of the different sorts of supplier. The former has a very high management overhead as it will typically require many interviews to get the people you need. (a 10 to 1 ratio is often required.) However, once the first good contractor with the required expertise is in place, they can help recruit the others. The danger to watch for is a temptation on the part of the contractor to recruit mediocre people so as to make their position more secure.

Engaging a supplier is very much a mixed blessing. While it can save the recruitment overhead and provide you with the expertise you need, it will tend to be more expensive and will require considerably more management. How much will depend on the type of supplier you engage and what you have engaged them to do. If they have been engaged on a resource enhancement basis then they should supply experienced people that complement the existing staff and be managed in the same way. There will be arguments about how many of them you need and whether they have enough of the experience required, but once this is agreed things usually settle down. This resource is usually contracted on a 'time & materials' basis. Many suppliers don't like this approach as they see it as the client 'cherry picking' their best people. They also feel it makes their staff vulnerable to being mismanaged by the client, for example being over demanding or directing their staff incorrectly. With this approach the supplier has technically no responsibility with respect to delivery – though if the project is a failure they will still suffer reputational damage.

If, however, the supplier has been engaged on some form of 'fixed price' basis i.e. they have quoted a price to deliver an agreed set of functionality, then management of them actually becomes much more difficult and the overhead higher. It is also likely to be more expensive, not least because the supplier will have included a high contingency in their quotation in order to cover their risk of underestimating the cost.

The high management overhead comes from a whole range of things including –

• The inevitably antagonistic nature of an engagement based on a legal contract. It may not start off like that but very often ends up that way.
• The management of 2 effectively separate teams (in-house staff and supplier staff and how they do *or don't* work together).
• The need to ensure that the requirements are sufficiently robust (they won't be) to meet contractual obligations.
• Managing permanent staff who are unhappy and resentful because they feel they have been effectively excluded from an important project.
• Trying to ensure that the expertise which is developed as part of the project is somehow transferred

to the (unhappy and resentful) permanent staff.

So often companies think that engaging a supplier on a fixed price contract somehow means that they can put their feet up and the supplier will do all the work. They think that they don't have any responsibility for the project if it fails. Nothing could be further from the truth on both counts. Managing a fixed price contract requires a very significant management overhead and a great deal of skill and experience if it is not going to degenerate into squabbling. In the worst cases it can even end up in court (which would require even more skills and experience!). If the project does fail, then the permanent staff will be blamed for not selecting or managing the supplier correctly.

This problem can occur when the Commercial department do the procurement without the people who have to actually manage those resources being sufficiently involved. There can be a sort of 'fire and forget' attitude from the Commercial department who assume that once they have a signed contract that their work is done.

Things to look for.

A sure sign of resources not being selected purely on merit is when the same faces keep appearing on the best projects no matter what skills required are. If the person making the appointments in this way is challenged they will tend to try and justify their selection by saying things like – "For this project I thought that "X" was what was needed." When "X" is some skill only vaguely related to that needed on the project but which just happens to be what their best mate has. Suppliers do a form of this too of course. Having sold their company to you on the grounds that they have unlimited resource in every possible skill set, the same (often very junior) people keep turning up no matter what the project is.

Another bad sign is decisions being made in order to accommodate particular resources. To a degree there is nothing wrong with this. If the company has expertise in certain products for example, then why not use that product? The problem comes when the product is actually unsuitable and its *only* merit is that there is existing expertise in it.

If your Commercial department or the people contracting with a supplier for a fixed price engagement seem to be doing so in an apparently relaxed manner, then be concerned. If they don't check that the references given by the potential supplier are actually genuine, and have mandated that you will be provided with at least some of their most experienced staff, then be very concerned.

What to do about it ?

The problem with cliques, like the ones who hog the best projects, is that they are very hard to shift once they are established. The damage they do is at least twofold. Firstly, they are very bad for morale because other staff feel they are being unfairly treated. Secondly, they also reduce the total competence of the organization by allowing expertise to be concentrated into too small a group. To stop this happening requires that people outside of the clique must insist more on being part of the best projects. Many people will find this difficult to do but if even one or two of the best people manage it based on their recognised competence, and then insist on pulling others with them, then it can be achieved.

Engaging on a fixed price basis with suppliers is very difficult and requires excellent management skills and very good commercial expertise. If this type of contract has not been used successfully before, then it should be approached with great caution. It should not be used for the first time on a high profile or very important project. It is better to practice on a low profile, low priority, low risk project first. With a suitable Guinea pig, ensure that the contract is drawn up following discussions not just with the Commercial and IT departments but as wide a group of stakeholders as possible. This will help ensure not only that the best, most complete contract is drawn up, but that everyone involved in the project understands it and can help manage it.

Put a tick in the 'Poor Resourcing' box.

4. PLANS.

What is the issue ?

Plans have been mentioned frequently as one of the things that more conventional books on project management tend to cover extensively. It might seem therefore that it doesn't have a place in this book. Not so. This section is about the *way* people plan and how it causes problems.

As with so many other things, the importance of project plans varies depending upon the methodology being used. While whatever methodology you are using requires at least an over-arching plan, the really detailed planning is much more of a Waterfall requirement.

Two really relevant quotations on planning are – firstly, "Plans are bunk. *Planning* is everything." This is by D.W. Eisenhower (top US general and eventual US president). The second is, roughly (from the French) – "No plan survives contact with the enemy." (N. Bonaparte , top French general and eventual emperor of France.) Together they basically say – in the real world things change so you need to be prepared for that. You do this by really understanding what you are doing in the first place so that when change occurs you understand what is really happening and can respond to it.

Whether the fact that both these top planners went from army officer to running their country (or countries) is significant or not isn't known but it isn't something explored in this book.

The issue with plans is broadly either having no plan or having too much plan.

Having no plan at all is the worse situation. A plan has many purposes and letting people know what they should be doing is only one of them. The Eisenhower quote above illustrates that the main purpose is to really, really understand what needs done, when it is to be done, dependencies, resources needed etc. If this is properly understood then, as things change, they can be responded to and dealt with successfully.

Plans are also however, a key means of communication for a project. This is communication not just to the members of the team so that they know what they should be doing, and when, but what other people should be doing as well. The plan is also an important means of communication to project stakeholders and the wider organization so that they know what is (supposed) to be happening. If used properly the plan is also an important means of gaining and keeping the confidence of the organization that the project knows what it is doing, is being well run and is likely to succeed.

Not having a plan which provides all of the above will therefore put the project seriously at risk. It is unlikely however that a single version of the plan will be sufficient. Different views of the plan will be needed for different people – a very high level view for programme boards and senior stakeholders, much more detailed for project team members. They must, of course, be based on the same foundation.

Not quite as bad, at least initially, but still problematic, is the opposite situation i.e. <u>too much, too detailed planning</u>. Until the advent of planning software this was rarely a problem. Now it is possible to create massive, unwieldy and frankly fairly useless plans, running to thousands and thousands of highly inter-related tasks and activities which are almost worse than no plan at all. Indeed, as producing these takes up considerable specialist resource, they are often not worth the effort and in some ways can be counter-productive. They often result from having a specialist planning team. If planning is what you do, then there will be a tendency to make the plan as important i.e. big, as possible.

In the worst case, over-elaborate and complex plans not only fail to deliver on one of the key purposes - of providing good communication (because only the specialist few can really understand them) but can actually cause delays to the project as the team waits for the plan to be updated in response to a change. They can also hinder communication if the software used to produce these plans is not widely distributed in the organization due to cost and training issues. Too often a massively complex plan is presented to a senior level, such as a Programme Board, in the expectation that it will impress them. The opposite is usually the case. It is seen instead as another example of IT talking in a language that only they can understand.

Things to look for.

If there is no plan at all then that should be pretty obvious. But if signs of this are needed then look for arguments breaking out as people discover such things as - they don't know who is supposed to be developing what, or that resources they need to get their job done aren't there, or that the project budget is disappearing fast without much being produced. Under-planned projects can often get off to a fast start but it can't last and they quickly come grinding to a halt when the problems kick in.

On the other hand, if excessive plans are being produced the signs are, initially at least, very different. This can include a very slow start to the project as the mega-plan has not been finished. If the project has this kind of obsession with complex plans, team members will be forbidden from starting anything just in case it turns out to be the wrong thing when the plan is finally published. As the plan will run to 1000's and 1000's of lines, few people will understand it and there will be further delay as they try and work out what they are supposed to be doing. This pattern will be repeated on a regular basis when the plan needs to be updated – for example to reflect the fact that the project didn't start when the plan said it should.

The plan may actually impress the wider stakeholder group initially. It will be seen as a sign that the project seems to know what they are doing. This doesn't last however. Because it is such a poor communication tool, frustration grows at not being able to understand what is actually going on. Eventually, the over planned project can come to resemble the under-planned project in many ways – late, over budget and under delivering.

What to do about it ?

If the plan seems to have become an end in itself rather than a means to ensure that the project is being run efficiently, then it is counterproductive. A common reason for over planning is the inexperience of the project manager and the planning specialist. Their lack of confidence can lead to an over reliance on the plan, which they feel must be as detailed as possible. If the start of the project is stalled because the complete plan has not been finished, then the more experienced members of the team should produce their own mini-plans based on what they know can be started at very little or no risk.

If no plan has been published, and there doesn't seem to be any sign of one arriving any time soon, then the chances are it isn't being developed. In this circumstance enquiries from team members about a plan are often dismissed with a – "You know what you are doing, just get on with it." This is effectively the same situation as too much planning. As team members are unlikely to be able to force the issue, then as with too much planning, they will have to do their own. This may be very informal but discussing amongst themselves to agree what should be happening and when, can be very effective. One downside of this is that it confirms in the minds of some people that a plan wasn't needed!

More senior staff can also enquire about a plan and won't be dismissed in the same way. They tend to be fobbed off with a "It's nearly finished and will be issued shortly". This is when Project Bingo becomes useful. With a tick in the Plans box it not only informs everyone that the plan is a problem but it reminds the more senior staff member to follow up their request.

Put a tick in the Plans box.

5. MORALE.

What is the issue ?

Morale is quite a vague term. It is one of those things that everyone thinks they know what you mean, but might have trouble actually agreeing a definition. Everyone also agrees that it's important. What is meant here by it is that sense of confidence and optimism, usually founded on *realistic*, good self-esteem. In particular, it is one of the vital things that enables a person or team to persevere against adversity, to drive through to achieve objectives. It's importance is often talked about with respect to the military but it is also widely regarded as vital for sports teams.

As with any team sport, the performance of a project team is very affected by the morale of the team and the people in it. Yet if the performance of humans is so affected by this, why is it usually given so little attention on projects? While morale is widely recognised as important, only a very occasional and superficial lip-service is usually paid to it by most managers on their project. This is typical of people who don't know much about how to manage people but have vaguely heard about this morale thing.

The fundamental problem for many project managers is that they don't really give much thought to what good morale is and how to achieve it. Then, when the inevitable difficulties emerge on the project, the team isn't able to respond as well as it could. In most cases individuals are expected to achieve their own good morale and, if they don't, then that is considered to be a failure on their part.

Things to look for.

The worst case is when nothing whatever is done to achieve and maintain good morale. Even the most basic good practice such as project initiation or team meetings are ignored. The project is effectively being run as a loose collection of individuals who just happen to have to talk to each other occasionally. When things start to go wrong, as they will, the situation is met by a sense of puzzlement and confusion. A typical question such as, "Why are people not just sorting this out, why is this such a problem ?", will often literally be asked by management who think their job is mainly just to attend the most important meetings.

If there is even a little recognition of the need for good morale, then a common response consists of doing things that is thought will make people 'happy' – however temporarily. These can be characterised as things which are easy (and ideally, cheap) to do and certainly don't require any real interaction with staff. An example would be when an undercurrent of poor morale or even discontent is (finally) detected and so a beer night or something similar is arranged. It may make the team happier in the very short term (i.e. until the next morning), but it will not improve the fundamentals. Indeed, as some will see it for what it is – a poor attempt to paper over the real problems, it may even make things worse.

There is also the situation where there are some minor efforts to achieve good morale but they are done badly or insufficiently. As a result, morale will be moderate and may well be good enough for most projects but will collapse if a major problem occurs. These efforts would include attempts at good comms, or some recognition of individuals need for career development. Unfortunately, there will continue to be a lack of the fundamentals of good management, such as actually treating staff as intelligent adults or involving people in decision making.

However, the most obvious sign of poor morale is the degree of low level complaining by staff amongst themselves. A certain amount of this will occur on even the best run projects as it is almost a basic human need. One way that the degree of this can be judged is when there are many complaints about fairly trivial things which would otherwise not be remarked upon. If these trivial complains are also being raised in staff forums when they really don't seem important enough, this could well be an indication that, consciously or not, staff are expressing a deeper discontent. This is a sure sign that morale is a problem

What to do about it ?

The definition of good morale used here - that it is based on confidence, optimism and good self-esteem, has to be the starting point for improving bad morale. While, of course, individuals have a responsibility for themselves, there is so much that management can do. Fundamentally, it is the way that management treat staff that is a major determinant in how staff feel about themselves. Simplistically, if treated badly, staff will either assume that they aren't very good and perform poorly, or react against this by rejecting this characterisation and rejecting management authority as well. Either of which is bad for the project.

People who work on projects are usually amongst the best and brightest their company has available. Yet, too often, management treat them as if the opposite was the case. Examples would be, announcing things which staff know to be untrue but assuming that staff aren't smart enough to work this out or justifications for decisions which are clearly wrong, and expecting them to be believed. Some of the things which are too rarely done by poor management which would help achieve good morale, are the following :-

• Let staff know why they are doing what they are doing and that what they are doing is valuable.

• Talk to staff as mature adults who can tell when what they are being told is bullshit.

• Involve, when possible, staff in decision making. They are the ones who have to implement these decisions and will do it much better if they understand why that decision was made - even if they don't agree with it. In particular, staff need to know that decisions are not being made by senior management for purely personal reasons.

• Don't try and bribe staff. It is impossible to bribe

everyone, so those that aren't offered are resentful, and those that are, don't stay bribed for very long. Don't expect something trivial such as a few drinks to have much effect. It also causes dissention in the team.

- Staff know that the objectives of the project will take priority but rightly expect that their needs, especially career needs, are met at least to some degree. Even just *trying* to do this will be recognised and appreciated by staff.

- Manage all the team – not just the more senior members. Even the most junior member of the team really wants the project to be a success. Even though they know they will not get the same credit for success as more senior members, winning is always better. No one really wants to be associated with failure.

- Good comms – tell people what is going on. It is rarely the case that people can be told everything there is to know, but they need to know that they are at least being told what they *can* be told.

Put a tick in the Bad Morale box.

6. SCOPE CREEP.

What is the issue ?

It is widely recognised that the single biggest cause of project failure is scope creep i.e. the changing of the objectives of a project. This almost always means adding more. You could refine that statement by saying that scope creep is the biggest of causes *actually measured*. It is only true for projects which are managed using a variant of the 'Waterfall' methodology, as the focus on these projects is scope. If we accept that, whatever the actual percentage, scope creep is a significant problem on many projects, then it should be identified and dealt with. However, to be more specific, this component is about **badly managed** scope change. Change which has been handled correctly i.e. through a proper, formal change management process should not cause a project to fail.

One problem with managing scope creep is identifying when it is occurring. As a project progresses, (and again this is mainly for Waterfall projects), a great deal of effort is focussed on clarifying what is to be delivered. As the scope usually wasn't very clear to begin with, how do we know whether it has changed or not ? Only the most obvious cases tend to be *easily* identified as scope creep. Typically there are endless arguments occurring within the project team and with users/stakeholders on what is, and isn't, already included in the scope. These arguments are usually lost by the project team.

The reasons that scope change occurs are varied. Sometimes the changes are for 'good' reasons.

It could be that there has been a change in company strategy or policy. It could be that upon further analysis the original scope is realised to be no longer possible or to have too little benefit. In these cases it would obviously be wrong to simply carry on as before. More often however, scope is not changed for good reasons. The most common is that those responsible for defining the scope for the business neglected to include something they should have. This occurs far more frequently than it ought to. Mainly this is because the people with the responsibility for this have no experience of doing it. They are not aware, for example, of how important it usually is to get it very right, first time. It is, of course, the role of the Business Analyst to work with them to ensure that this happens, but it is never perfect.

One of the ways that scope creep occurs is when an individual in the project decides to include something as part of their personal agenda. This can happen at different levels on the project. It could be the inclusion of a new technology, that wasn't originally part of the scope, because someone wants to get experience of it. It could also be the inclusion of whole new areas of business functionality because the programme director wants the additional status and budget that it brings.

This is usually done without proper consideration of the consequences – because that would draw attention to it. Adding a new technology for example doesn't just involve the cost of the technology itself but also the cost of training staff and the loss of productivity to the project while they become proficient in it. If this technology is additional to an existing one, rather than a straight replacement, then there are additional software maintenance and support costs, including that of a more complex architecture. Less tangible, is the impact on staff who have an additional technology to cover.

Adding whole new areas of functionality is rarely done without at least a budget to go with it (it is just too big an item). What is usually ignored, or at least downplayed, is the management overhead that the extra scope brings with it. This is often dismissed as something the project manager can cope with simply by working (even) longer hours. However, even if the project manager can (and perhaps more importantly) wants, to work longer hours, it will have a negative impact on the project as a whole as their focus is more thinly spread. On top of this is the impact on other members of the team – who may not have signed up for this entirely wholeheartedly.

There are also scope changes which happen because they are asked for by a friend of someone on the project – 'mates changes'. While these tend to be small changes which can be included with relatively little impact, they do set a bad standard of behaviour, which can easily get out of control.

Probably the worst sort of changes are those that are imposed on the project by someone very senior in the organization. These tend to come down from on-high in the form of a question such as – "I have just discovered that 'X' isn't in scope, why is that?". This is usually followed very soon after with a 'request' that 'X' be included. As this person is very senior, the management of the project team will immediately rush to include whatever it is that has been asked for. This is done partly out of a misplaced sense of embarrassment for not having included it in the first place when it was *obviously* something which should have been. It is also because they think/know it will affect their career if they don't. Unfortunately it is the whole team that suffers by trying to accommodate something that wasn't budgeted or resourced for. These changes also have a tendency to be on the large size because very senior people don't 'do' small things.

Of course, if the project then fails despite the project team working very hard to include these new things, it is not the very senior person who will get the blame.

Things to look for.

No help is needed to identify big changes to scope as it is obvious to all that they have happened. At the very least the reworking of plans and activities will make this clear. Unfortunately, sometimes there will be an attempt to pretend that there hasn't been a change and therefore no effort is made to change any of the project artefacts. This can be more than a little bizarre and will always end in someone's tears. Importantly, the changes will not go through any Change Management process.

It is likely that the majority of changes will be relatively small. However, if these are in large enough numbers they will still have the potential to be just as devastating to a project as a major change. Identifying these is more difficult as they typically occur at a low level, on a day to day basis. Some of these are inevitable as the process of scope clarification is gone through and initial misunderstanding are identified and resolved.

However, there will also be changes where an attempt is made to slip them through without them being identified as such. This is because the people involved are embarrassed by what was actually an error of omission in the first place. The people who will identify these changes are the Developers who are now being asked to do more than was originally budgeted for. They don't usually require much encouragement to flag up that changes have occurred – at least amongst themselves.

What to do about it ?

This is obviously mainly an issue for scope driven projects – which of course, the majority are. One solution therefore is not to do scope driven projects! Some projects are not suitable for an Agile methodology so this is not always an option unfortunately. This then becomes an issue of governance.

How to ensure that proposed or attempted scope increases are properly governed ? There are obvious ways via the project boards (or whatever your equivalent) and things like external reviews. If these are proving ineffective then it becomes important that the other members of the project use their voice to do what they can. The impact on these people is most immediately on their workload and their ability to cope with the additional scope. They should have an already agreed full workload so pushing back on anything additional should be straightforward – if the project has been planned properly. In some organisations of course, staff are too cowed to feel able to push back as it will affect their career.

This section is about badly managed scope change. The simple solution is therefore to ensure that all significant change is managed through a proper Change Management process. This should include assessing the impact of a proposed change in the first instance, before it goes through any formal governance. If the change is subsequently accepted into the scope of the project then both the budget and the plan must also change. While this is obvious, it may not be popular with very senior people, (speaking truth to power never is), but simply pointing out that you are following the company process should make it do-able. As the alternative is a failed project, it is surely better to have a short period of relative unpopularity rather than the longer term negativity of being associated with a project failure.

On scope focussed projects ensuring clarity of the requirements is so vital that the resources assigned to this task must be of the highest possible level of expertise. Very few projects get all of the resources that they want so this must be one of the areas to be prioritised.

When the relatively small changes are identified it is important that the standard for dealing with these is set from the earliest possible point in the project. Anything which is going to impact the project budget or plan must be formally dealt with – whether the change is for 'good' or 'bad' reasons. Personal embarrassment cannot be allowed to dictate how the project is managed. If attempts to circumvent this are identified, and stopped firmly as soon as possible, then the standard for the project will be quickly set.

Put a tick in the Scope Change box.

7. QUALITY of IT MANAGEMENT.

What is the issue ?

This book is subtitled - 'Why humans can't do projects', but is this true of all humans or just IT people? (We would probably have to include Engineers in this 'can't do' group as engineering projects have an as bad, or even worse, delivery record). Is there something unique about IT people that causes IT projects to fail ?

It has been said that a good proportion of people who work in IT are "definitely on the autism scale". That might well account for the often poor interpersonal and hence management skills. However, that characteristic tends to be only true of people in the technical roles. There are many others such as Project Managers, Business Analysts, Content Designers and Testers who are quite adept at the softer skillsets. Indeed, it a true-ism in IT that projects very rarely fail because of the technology or for technical reasons, which is where the technical roles operate and make the decisions.

Perhaps it is the IT environment which is to blame? It is one which is subject to unrelenting change and as a result requires constant decision making. For example, the stream of new technologies that could potentially be used generates many major and minor questions such as –

- Which of these technologies are suitable for *this* particular company ?

- Is this latest thing just hype or could it be a real benefit ?
- Is it the right version for this situation ?

Inevitably some bad decisions are going to be made. However, this would not explain the high project failure rate. As mentioned previously, the 'wrong' choice of technology is not often the reason for project failure. It may result in a less than perfect solution or one which might not have the longevity another choice might have had. (Most businesses would be more than happy with a service which 'only' lasted 5 years. Indeed, if it was actually a good service in the first place, which had been delivered on time and to budget, they would be very happy indeed.)

In fact, as many technologies have matured, the choice between products has often become even less critical. It is quite common, for example, for the choice between the top 3 or 4 products to be mostly insignificant. So, it seems unlikely therefore that the too technical focus of some IT people is, in itself, the cause of so many failures.

The sense remains however that the quality of management in IT is poor. Looking more generally, it is all too often the case, that IT departments are not happy, well run functions. This is despite the fact that IT staff are doing a job of their own choice, that is usually well paid, has great opportunities for promotion, to change employer easily etc. Perhaps the biggest indictment of IT management is the usually low esteem in which the IT Department is held by the rest of the organisation. Given the critical importance that IT has to most organisations, and increasingly in peoples personal lives, IT should be appreciated and respected, if not exactly loved. Finance departments have managed it.

The issue is that while IT departments exist fundamentally to manage technology, they often focus on that to the exclusion of other areas of management. The resulting generally poor quality of management affects projects – because staff are not the happy, highly motivated and efficient team they should be.

Things to look for.

One of the reasons for the poor level of general management in IT is that so little training in it is done. This is partly because it is not regarded as being very important but also because there is so much other, technical, training to be done. Training budgets are never unlimited and priorities will be set. An example of this low priority is that it is rare in a job interview to be asked what training has been done, or what qualifications achieved, in general management. A lack of sufficient emphasis on, or even the option to do, general management training, is therefore a likely sign of poor management.

This excessive focus on the technical aspects is also illustrated by the poor record that IT departments tend to have in relation to management activities such as Annual Performance Appraisals. Typically, if statistics are published in an organisation on what percentage of appraisals each departments has completed, the IT department is at or near the bottom (usually fighting it out with Finance for last spot).

One of the most damaging symptoms of poor management skills is that IT directors so often are not members of the most senior board in an organisation. Given the importance of IT to most organisations this shouldn't be the case and it reflects both poor management skills and a lack of political ability. Given its importance, IT directors should be able to work their way to the most senior levels.

A lack of engagement with the wider company and an over emphasis on the technical is also reflected in the insular nature of many IT departments. This can be seen in poor involvement in company activities such as social events, supporting charitable activities or volunteering for companywide projects. It is also reflected in the use of a language that people outside of IT do not understand. Most specialists have a vocabulary of their own but use it only amongst themselves. IT however are always being criticised for being incomprehensible – even those whose job it is to work with other departments. The use of an exclusive language, without recognising that that is what is happening, is another bad sign.

What to do about it ?

There is a balance to be struck between achieving and maintaining the very high level of technical expertise required by the IT function, and the more general management skills needed to run a department and engage fully with the wider organisation. Particularly during periods of rapid change in technology (which is pretty much almost always) it will be difficult to focus on anything other than that. However, this doesn't excuse the more senior IT managers from both ensuring that those staff whose job it is to manage staff, and they themselves, receive the training necessary to do that aspect of their job well.

Individuals can also take responsibility for their own career by insisting on achieving the necessary balance between technical and non-technical training. There was a time when the concept of the 'hybrid manager' was very fashionable. This was an attempt to introduce a better balanced manager into IT – people who were not too focussed on the technology, who would have a better understanding of the business they worked in and be able to engage better with non-IT colleagues. It didn't seem to come to much. The concept was a good one and would be a relatively quick way to improve management skills in IT departments. The problem is however – how do you persuade good managers to join the IT Department !

Put a tick in the Quality box.

8. FEAR as a MANAGEMENT TOOL.

What is the issue ?

Using fear to manage staff is not the exclusive preserve of project managers, but it is much too common. It is used more often than not because the individual doesn't have the managerial skills or the confidence to do anything else. It is unfortunately what too many people think is the default way of doing things i.e. that is how managers are supposed to behave. There are also people who just have a character flaw which causes them to exploit the position of power they are in.

The fear that is generated comes mainly from the threat of being dismissed from the project. Getting rid of an employee from a company has varying degrees of difficulty. However, it is much easier to remove a project team member, as staff come and go on a project throughout its life cycle. Removing someone before their original planned time is therefore relatively easy. This may not be as serious for the individual as it would be in a permanent role but it is serious enough to damage a career – and staff know it.

A manager who uses fear to manage staff is creating two main problems. Firstly, the direct reports of the manager will almost certainly perform less than their best because very few people respond well to this form of behaviour. As these are the most senior members of the team this will be a serious problem. Secondly, a culture of bullying is created within the team. Other members of the team will take their lead from the manager and behave in the same way. Very quickly the whole project is performing badly due to poor communication, lack of support, sullen resistance etc. When the project is finished it is likely that the members of the team will be exhausted and highly stressed and unlikely to perform well in their next assignment. They may also carry over behaviours which are unproductive and at odds with the general company culture.

Things to look for.

It isn't always the case that this type of manager is prone to shouting and threatening. Indeed, if the manager is aware that this type of behaviour is frowned upon, they may appear outwardly to be very pleasant. Nevertheless, the signs are not that subtle. The approach is basically that of a dictator and this will include :-

- Not allowing any real discussion on decisions, expecting them to be accepted uncritically.
- Dismissing or overruling any proposals from staff – often just to reinforce their own authority.
- Ignoring issues until they are critical and they have no choice but address them. Then blaming someone else.
- Surrounding themselves with people who agree uncritically with everything they say.
- Being very quick to criticise others, ignoring the context, and punishing (e.g. reducing someone's responsibilities) very quickly.
- Being very quick to take full credit for anything

that goes even slightly well and not recognising the contribution of others.
- Formal processes will often be ignored as they prefer to be able to dictate their personal preference.

If this is the type of manager you have on your project then you will probably not need much help to identify it.

What to do about it ?

The obvious thing to do would be to report the behaviour to the persons line manager. However, these people are usually quite clever at ensuring that this behaviour is not visible to their manager and it may not therefore be believed. It is also unfortunately true that in many organisations doing this would not be well received. It forces senior management to do something about it which they are too often reluctant to do. It is also the case that in too many organisations this type of behaviour is accepted as necessary to 'get the job done'.

The alternative is to use the power that staff have on the project. This is not to suggest going on strike, but rather that the most irreplaceable individuals on the project use that power to push back on these behaviours. Those with the scarcest skills or most valuable knowledge can do anything from simply insisting on formal processes being followed, to making clear that they are looking for another project because of this behaviour. At the extreme, they could also actually leave the company, making clear why they are doing so.

Staff will often persevere on these projects because they think that the skills or knowledge they are gaining makes it worthwhile. This can sometimes be true, but too often the majority of the credit for the project within the organisation is taken by the manager and the emotional damage from the bullying outweighs any technical skills gained.

Put a tick in the 'Fear' box.

9. BAD COMMUNICATION.

What is the issue ?

One of the reasons why humans have achieved much of what we have, is because of our communication abilities. This has allowed us to, amongst other things, organize in groups efficiently, making the most of our abilities, and minimising our weaknesses. As a result we have been able to do such things as organize to build huge and complex structures, or progressively add to previous learning and achievements.

Good communication is vital if any sort of team activity is going to work well and not degenerate into chaos. This must include such things as a common language, clarity of objectives, universally understood ways of working, with an agreed sets of tools. With respect to language, this must also include the jargon that IT is very inclined to create, ensuring clarity of meaning. Because there are usually no formal definitions of what these IT terminologies mean, this often causes confusion not just within IT but even more so within the wider project team and the organisation generally.

Unfortunately, very little effort tends to go into good communications. It might consist of regular reporting to the appropriate committees, with perhaps something less detailed to a wider audience. However, too often, after the initial effort, even this fades as the pressure of other aspects of the project takes hold.

There is a 'law' (IT has lots of 'laws') which states that the more people there are on a project, the more likely it is to fail. This may seem counterintuitive as surely the more people you have available on a project to do the work the more likely it is to deliver? Isn't the usual problem that a project doesn't have *enough* people?

The basis for this 'law' is that, on projects, good communication is vital - because of the large number of interdependencies to be managed for example. This requires a management overhead if it is to be achieved at the correct level. This overhead increases exponentially as the number of people to be communicated with increases. As a result, as the size of a project grows, communication tends to get progressively more difficult. If more managers are added to reflect the size of the team and maintain good communication, they themselves become part of the problem as *they* have to be communicated with as well.

Eventually, with enough people, the point is reached where, in reality, there won't be just one project – it will naturally separate into several smaller projects teams. If the project has been organised in this way at the beginning and an appropriate structure put in place, this could work. However, if it happens in an unplanned, unmanaged way, the most likely result is chaos.

It has been claimed that no good software has been created by a team of more than 3 people. The justification for this was that the logic, and consistency of style and standards – the quality of the software, couldn't be maintained. There is an element of truth in this. Certainly there are many large in-house developed systems and commercial packages, which were developed by a cast of 1000's, which are of very poor quality.

Given that most people realise how important good communication is it is odd how little effort goes into achieving it. For example, too often a problem is dismissed as 'a communication problem', as if that was somehow inevitable and therefore 'ok'. This is almost never followed up with an attempt to do something to improve communication. Very often the problem was actually nothing to do with communication at all but, for example, blatantly caused by bad behaviour on someone's part. Yet it seemed ok to blame it on 'poor communication' as if that somehow couldn't be helped. An example of humans avoiding the real issues.

Things to look for.

If you join a project and discover that you are one of hundreds or even thousands then you should be immediately concerned. If the project governance does not appear to understand the importance of good communication and how the <u>structure needs to reflect and support</u> this, then you should be very concerned.

If you discover only *accidently* things you needed or wanted to know, then amongst other things, there is almost certainly a systemic comms problem.

If budget is spent on glossy posters etc. which don't actually say much, or if the main means of communication with the team is via email (one up from telepathy, but only just), or if the comms which is produced is so out of date that everyone already knows what's in it, then there is certain to be a problem.

If there are multiple misunderstandings at project board level about things like - what the actual status of the project is, or who is actually responsible for which things, then the project will not get the support it needs and is at serious risk.

If poor quality management - bad decision making for example, is blamed on poor communication then this indicates the low level of importance that is given to communication. This implies that people think it is sort of ok to have bad communication.

What to do about it ?

Projects need to include achieving good communication, in all their planning and organization, from the very start. If this isn't achieved from the beginning it is very difficult to fix once the project is progressing. Even if communication is improved after a bad start, significant damage may have been done to many aspects of the delivery of the project, to the morale of the team and to the wider perception of the project.

If possible, there should be people dedicated to producing good comms. This must include removing, or at least translating, any jargon. The dedicated comms people should also find out what the project team, and wider stakeholder group, actually want to know about. The comms materials produced should then be, at least in part, based on this.

As much face to face communication with all levels of management should be achieved as possible. Project members must be given the opportunity to ask questions and get <u>real</u> answers. This is time consuming for the project but is a very worthwhile investment.

Put a tick in the "Bad Communication " box.

10. IGNORE the BUSINESS CASE.

What is the issue ?

This issue is the practice of producing a business case, then ignoring it. It was discussed earlier that one of the main reasons that projects fail is the increase in or significant change of scope. Some of the reasons *why* this happens were discussed. One of the key *ways* in which this is allowed to happen is to conveniently ignore the business case for a project.

The business case broadly defines the scope of a project and imposes a discipline based on what the 'right' (for the company) things are to do. This is usually based on the economic benefits of the different elements of scope. By ignoring the business case a project will find it easier to wander off and do whatever it feels like doing. This is very true of the Waterfall methodology based project where the business case gets produced at the beginning of the project, but then increasingly forgotten about as time goes on. It is also true for Agile methodology based projects where doing a 'mini' business case for each sprint becomes a bit too tedious and is seen as slowing the pace.

However it is done, the end result is a project which is unlikely to achieve the objectives that the company had planned and certainly not the benefits that were hoped for. Even if the project is not seen as an outright failure there will be disappointment and a subsequent loss of confidence, not least in the project team.

Things to look for.

Perhaps the first clue that the business case is not going to be the focus it should be, comes when it is first being drawn up. If done properly, each major component of the scope will have a business sponsor who is responsible for ensuring that the scope is clear and benefits accurately defined. The sponsor should also be responsible for ensuring that the benefits forecast are actually achieved. For that reason, this should be someone who really wants the project deliverables for their area of the business.

If this sponsor is not in place but the costs and benefits are put together in isolation by, for example, a Business analyst only, then it will be all too easy for the project to drift from the original scope. As difficulties arise and if there is no sponsor digging their heals in and insisting on achieving the original scope, it is very tempting to jettison difficult items for something easier to achieve.

Another warning sign that the business case is likely to be ignored is if there is no regular financial reporting against the original case. This should happen at the regular project board updates. If this doesn't happen then, again, it is too easy for scope to alter over time. If this reporting isn't happening it is also likely that the necessary preparation for the adoption of the new system by the business isn't happening either. The forecast benefits are therefore unlikely to be achieved.

A typical danger point for when the original business case might be conveniently forgotten is if there is a significant change in technology. For example, if new technology has been planned but upon more detailed examination it is found that it isn't as capable as first thought. There will be great temptation to alter the scope in order to fit in with the capabilities of the new technology – not least to avoid IT's embarrassment. If the difference is serious enough, this would mean a major revision of the project and re-doing the business case.

The above examples primarily describe a situation where the scope of a project is being reduced in some way. In fact, by far the most common occurrence is for attempts to be made to increase scope. There is nothing wrong with this exactly – what is important is how it is managed. An increase in scope is almost certain to require additional time and resources for the project and hence a revision of the business case. If this isn't done, and properly approved, the result is at best massive pressure on the project team to deliver more with the same resources. More likely, is a project that fails because it doesn't have the resources it needs. A sign that a badly managed scope increase is happening is when the new activity starts to get included in discussions of what is to be delivered without it going through any of the proper, formal processes of assessment and adoption.

What to do about it ?

It is in everyone's interest to properly manage

and adhere to the business case. Even projects which apparently finish successfully, but which have, in reality, only done so by reducing scope without updating the business case, are still damaging. The forecast benefits will not be achieved and the perception of at least partial failure within the organisation will result in a loss of confidence and belief in the ability to deliver. Projects where the scope has been increased, but the business case not revised, account for the majority of all project failures.

The simplest solution, when a change of scope is proposed, is to simply say – "Ok, but we need to do a quick revision of the business case". Individuals who try and resist this are usually doing so for personal reasons and are putting the project at risk.

Put a tick in the Business Case box.

11. BAD ORGANIZATION.

What is the issue ?

In this case, 'Bad Organization' means an organization structure which is not the most efficient for a project, but rather which serves another (usually political) end. An example of this would be when different roles or even functions are not directly managed by the project but rather operate in a sort of sub-contract or outsourced manner.

Projects that work best are those where everyone works together irrespective of where they have come from in the organization – they 'leave their badges at the door'. In this scenario everyone contributes their particular expertise for the common good of the project. Inter-departmental rivalry is non-existent, or at least, is at a minimum. However, there does still need to be clear lines of responsibility.

Decisions need to be made which are often messy in nature and which, inevitably, some will disagree with. However, the project will not succeed if some in the project head off in one direction and others in another. It is the role of the project or delivery manager to ensure that these decisions get made and that they are implemented. The organization of the project must support this.

There are a whole range of specialism on a project such as Business Analyst, UX or Technical Architect. These roles require considerable training and experience and are rightly extremely influential in the decision making process. It is important that their expertise is retained on a project and that they contribute fully when necessary. A certain degree of professional objectivity or separation is necessary in order to do this but, without becoming too purist.

It is the responsibility of the project or delivery manager to ensure that the objectives of the project are met within the parameters that have been set e.g. cost, scope, time scales etc., by managing the different inputs. It is essential therefore that all who are key to the success of the project are under the direct responsibility of the project manager for the duration of their time on the project. Projects with organizations which do not have that clear line of responsibility will be subject to indecision and lack of direction.

It can be argued that this approach is unnecessary as roles can contribute effectively without becoming a direct part of the team. However, as being a clear part of the project team is the simplest, most obvious, and most effective way to organize, the question must be – why do it any other way? It can only be for 'political', ego or other non-productive reasons.

A key example of the effect of separation on a project is when IT Operations staff (by this I mean primarily the Infrastructure function) are not an integral part of the project. The work that needs to be done to set up new environments, install software etc., becomes massively more difficult if it is being done remotely. Good communications becomes much more difficult to achieve so that anything which isn't defined and specified in the finest detail has the potential to become contentious. Attempts at flexibility or responsiveness tend to fail not just due to the bureaucratic nature of the interaction but because of the defensive positions that the different teams will tend to adopt as a default. If, for example, an IT Ops deliverable doesn't arrive when it is needed it becomes an issue of dispute as to whose fault it is. Importantly, attempts to recover the situation start much later than would otherwise be the case because time is wasted as people argue about who is to blame.

Things to look for.

The most obvious, physical sign of a fractured organisation is when the team are not co-located. While this is often just not possible due to office space restrictions, some attempt to get as many people as possible together should be made. This doesn't have to involve completely randomly spreading different roles around - different roles can still sit together.

The single most important sign of a bad organisation is when reporting lines are still back to the original team. If the direction of the activities of staff is not the responsibility of the project or delivery manager then problems will occur. Staff will always be looking to their permanent line manager for direction and non-project objectives or other priorities will quickly creep in. In addition, when the project is hit with difficulties too much management time will be taken up by meetings between the line managers of the different groups to sort things out.

What to do about it ?

A good example of a solution to the Bad Organisation problem is the introduction of DevOps. There are varying models of what this is, but even at its most simple (IT Ops staff being assigned temporarily for the duration of the project to work as an integral part of the team), it is very effective. It removes the deadening bureaucracy and the 'Them vs Us' mentality which often exists between Development and Operations. This illustrates very well the basic principle of the need for an organisation which is most efficient for the *project* rather than one which suits the *management* of the organisation.

This approach does have some difficulties however. Every project has to balance the needs of staff for professional development while also delivering the objectives of the project. (Problems of morale will quickly develop otherwise.) Unbelievable as it may seem, Project managers have been known to want to focus too much on the project objectives, to the exclusion of all else!

For this reason staff, while on the project, need to retain their links to whoever is responsible for their profession in the organisation. This could be either a 'Head of Profession', or if this doesn't exist, their line manager. While this is not for day to day management, it ensures that the correct balances are achieved and that the project benefits by ensuring that the quality of the work done on the project is up to standard.

Staff appraisals can be a problem if not worked

out between the different managers involved. The various annual objectives should be set by the line manager as normal, with a contribution by the project manager of the persons project objectives. This is when the right balance should be achieved. The appraisals themselves should still be done by the line manager but with major input from the project manager – even attending the meetings if that is sensible.

Put a tick in the "Bad Organisation' box.

12. TEAM BUILDING.

What is the issue ?

There are two aspects to this – first actually putting together the right people (i.e. skills and experience) to deliver the project successfully, and second getting them to work to their full potential **as a team**. Doing either of these badly is going to seriously affect the project. Not only will the lack of necessary skills cause delays and poorly developed systems but poor team working can quickly degenerate into inter-project rivalries as people start to look after their own interests.

It is rare in the real world for a manager to actually get all of the resources that they want. It is part of their job therefore to find a way to deliver successfully with less than what they think they really need. The first question they must answer is – what *are* the right resources for this particular project ? Usually the main danger is to rely too much on people you know and have worked with previously. Unless they have a very close fit to the skills profile needed, the project will be missing potentially vital expertise. Identifying all the right skills and how much of it is needed is therefore most likely to require input from a range of people – especially those with expertise in new areas.

The second aspect of this issue is bringing the resources together to build a high performing team. IT people tend to be a little more cynical than the norm –

perhaps from having been on the receiving end of too many routine, 'by the numbers', 'team building' exercises. The all too typical approach of – being sorted into small groups to discuss uninteresting subjects and produce bland responses to present back, is productive only if lunch is provided and is very, very good.

Things to look for.

The first thing to check is – do people know what they are doing? That may be a harsh way of looking at it but if aspects of the project are new – either technology, methodology or the business function, then unless enough expertise in the new things is brought onto the project, bad decisions and mistakes are almost certain to be made. This question must be answered based on the real experience people have rather than wishful thinking on their part.

If resource shortcomings are recognised, are sensible efforts being made to deal with them? Too many trainees will kill a project (though not as fast as choosing the wrong IT consultants). Also, if it is necessary, have real efforts been made to change the scope or timescales of the project to reflect the actual capability of the team ?

Is the team working well together ? Is communication good across the whole project ? Does it *feel* like a team ?

What to do about it ?

Having identified what resource is needed and secured what is available, the next step is filling any shortfall. The main option, adding resource from external sources is covered elsewhere. The other alternative is to train up existing staff in the missing skills. This is really something that all project managers should do, as part of every project they do, whether they have enough experienced staff or not. The key, sometimes critical, decision is – how much of a training overhead can this particular project take? The answer will depend upon circumstances such as –

- How many trainees are needed compared to existing experienced staff? Are the experienced staff good at providing this support? Can they cope with this and doing a delivery role?
- How critical is the project? If it is late due to taking on trainees, how bad will the impact be? Will the company understand and agree the late delivery?
- Is there a need for these skills in the long term? Is this investment in training therefore worthwhile?
- Is there sufficient training budget? What was allowed for in the project budget?

If neither external resource or the training of existing staff is an option, then the project itself must be looked at. Can the timescales or scope be changed to reflect the resources that are actually available? Embarking on a project that doesn't have the right resource and is therefore almost certain to fail is not in the best interests of either the team or the company.

If there are to be team building exercises then it is far better to have a relatively informal get together to really discuss the project. The agenda should be flexible enough so that it allows people to concentrate on the things which are actually important to them or that they really need to know. This could include - what the business objectives are, key criticalities, the technology and methodology to be used, understanding the project organisation, and how certain roles will work on the project.

In team building honesty is an extremely critical factor. If staff are honest about any lack of expertise, rather than bluffing for fear of losing a role on the project, then there is a good chance that proper measures can and will be taken to fix the problem.

If managers are honest in their dealings with staff and communicate with them as intelligent adults who are expert in their field, then real trust and respect will develop, which is the basis of good a team.

Put a tick in the 'Bad Team' box.

ENVIRONMENT ISSUES.

This section is concerned with the wider context within which a project exists. Projects would be so much easier and simpler if they could be delivered without having to consider anything but the technical or mechanical aspects. Unfortunately this is not so. Below are some of the main issues with which a project has to deal.

1. POLITICS.

What is the issue ?

'Politics' is sort of strange – everyone knows what it means but it is very hard to really define. Here it refers to all the non-productive, messy stuff that goes on in organizations but which everyone agrees really shouldn't. It is probably the root cause of more damage to projects than any other single thing. If what really causes most projects to fail is that people insist on giving in to their human weaknesses rather than simply delivering projects the way that the manual says they should, it is politics that is the most obvious general expression of those weaknesses.

Perhaps a better description of what is meant by politics in this sense is – the sum total of all of those interactions, of personal motives or non-project objectives, driven by usually unwritten or even unspoken policies and strategies. It would also include things like - actions which are designed to damage those considered to be rivals. So, for example, decisions are made which are not in the best interest of the project but are rather in the interests of an individual, or a group to which they belong. These decisions could include anything from - what the scope of the project will be, to project organisation, to who get what specific roles. The project can easily become the battleground on which political battles are fought with things such as project reporting, budgets and scope, the weapons used.

However much we might want an ideal world where there are no such politics, it doesn't exist. This is not least because there are individuals who use politics because they could not progress, or even survive, on ability alone. There are also too many individuals who want to, who enjoy, playing political 'games'. This needs to be recognised and managed.

Things to look for.

Sometimes political games are very upfront. This is especially true if the games are a result of competing groups and you happen to be, or are assumed to be, in one of them. You could be included in discussions about tactics against the competition for example.

More often the politics are a bit less blatant. One way to detect them is when things are being done which have no clear logic to them for the project. You have to suspect they are being done for ulterior motives.

Another indicator of politics at play is when the people who should be making the decisions don't seem to want to, for no apparent reason. The reason is often because they don't want to take responsibility for a decision which may have 'political' repercussions. Sometimes the responsibility is shirked by apparently innocently asking others their opinion on the issue. This opinion suddenly becomes *the* decision - much to the surprize of the person who expressed it. A variant of this is when decisions are left to the project technical team to make when they should be made by the business. (If the decision turns out to be 'wrong', it's just another example of IT telling the business what to do.)

What to do about it ?

As mentioned previously, unfortunately politics is something which will happen whether we like it or not. Given that, it has to be dealt with. This includes recognizing that decisions are not made in a technical 'vacuum', but will sometimes need to accommodate political considerations. So, how to get the right balance between the political and the technical ?.

There is, of course, no simple answer. However, there are some guiding principles which can help. The first of these is to remember that if the project fails then almost certainly no amount of managing the politics will compensate for that. At best it will minimise the damage to the individuals involved. Decisions must be made therefore with the good of the project as the highest priority. If there is a situation where there is a choice between choosing the 'political' option or the *only* correct 'technical' option, then the technical option must take priority.

A simple example of this might be the choice between technical products for the project. If one is favoured for political reasons (such as the supplier is well connected in the organization), but the product is not very suitable, then the decision must be to go with a more suitable product.

Making clear that decisions are very much evidence based will help to gain agreement from those who preferred the 'political' option. At the very least it means that people have to take responsibility for a decision not to choose the best solution. People rarely want to take that kind of risk.

It can also help to discuss the reasons for their non-selection with the supplier of this option. They should realise that choosing their product when it is unsuitable will damage their reputation, and so support your decision. (It has happened - there are some good suppliers out there, honestly!)

The above scenario is actually a fairly rare example of a binary decision. More common is that there are several products which are much the same (often the case in a mature market). In this situation there is no reason not to choose the product which will find political favour.

Even better is to avoid political arguments in the first place. Given that you know that politics can seriously affect the project, it is important to be as aware of what is happening as much as possible. This is not always easy given the focus that there needs to be on the delivery aspects of the project, but it is important. To that end, time must be made to find out what the political situation is. Using the previous example, it is best not to suddenly discover that a product has been initially chosen which is not favoured. If so, the project will be fighting a rear-guard action which it is less likely to win. Even if it does succeed in procuring its preferred solution, it might find that it has made enemies.

Time needs to be made therefore for the informal conversions through which the political situation can be understood. Again, using the same example, a few innocent conversations asking if people happen to have any preferences will quickly make clear if there is a political minefield or not. The same type of conversation with as wide a range of people as possible should be enough to understand the wider political landscape.

Probably the most difficult area, and the one most fraught with politics, is that of project scope. While this tends not to be as much of an issue on projects run on Agile principles, it can be a nightmare on projects using a 'Waterfall' methodology. As scope causes more project failures than anything else it is dealt with in a separate section. However, from a political point of view it is an excellent example of the need to understand, in advance, the wider situation. Knowing ahead of any meetings, what people are likely to ask for, and as importantly, why they want it, allows you to be prepared. The critical mistake is to allow the scope of the project to increase beyond the capability of the project to deliver it. Again, by being forewarned, it is much easier to reach agreement on an acceptable compromise.

However, it is important to remember that, while IT may provide input into scoping decisions, such as the estimates for each item, or advice on what areas most complement each other, the decisions themselves on what is included is for the business to make. Too often the difficult, political decisions are left to the project to make.

Put a tick in the Politics box.

2. TECHNOLOGY – WRONG CHOICE.

What is the issue ?

It was stated earlier that projects rarely fail because of the technology. (This is true – by far the biggest recorded cause of project failure is scope creep.) However, there are still some examples where the technology and the *management* of that technology is at the root of a projects problems.

The most obvious case is with the management of the selection of a new technology. If this is done badly and the wrong technology chosen this can have major consequences. Apart from the cost etc of the initial implementation, this can have detrimental effects for years beyond the first project. Even if this implementation manages to somehow achieve the desired objectives it is rare for that first instance to be all that is needed from the technology. Most systems are expected to last at least 5 years and most end up lasting much, much longer than that. If the wrong technology was chosen then every subsequent iteration will be more difficult, take longer and be more expensive.

Problems can occur if the implementation hasn't been properly prepared for. This can take a number of different forms. The most common is a failure to prepare staff for the new technology. There is a tendency to underestimate the amount of training required, how long it will take staff to become reasonably competent in the new tools and what support they need during this period. Some of this happens because suppliers will tend to talk up the ease of use and downplay the training etc, that is required. Until, that is, the product sale has been made and they are keen to sell other services, such as consultancy. Unfortunately, this will not have been included in the original project budget and so staff may get less help than they really need.

Another cause of technology related project failure is the integration of the new technology with that which is already installed. Most organizations today have highly complex and interdependent systems. These are usually composed of a combination of COTS (commercial off the shelf) packages and in-house developed systems. Some of these will have been developed long ago and often the software will not have been kept up to date.

It is not uncommon for the documentation to be non-existent and the knowledge of these systems to have left the organization many leaving 'do's' ago. So, when it comes to integrating a new product, there will be many problem areas, the impact of which tends to be underestimated until the project is well advanced.

There are also problems which can occur when it isn't new technology which is being implemented but rather new functionality on the current technology. As mentioned above, in most organizations the IT estate is made up of a very complex mixture, some of which is poorly understood. If that lack of knowledge isn't recognised then there can be a false confidence that the current technology is capable of doing the new things that are being asked of it. It can take some time before staff on the project finally accept that, actually, this isn't going to work. Some staff will also want to retain the old technology because that is their area of expertise and 'knowledge is power'.

Things to look for.

In all the examples above there is one common feature – a failure to properly analyse what is being asked of the technology and decide if the technology is actually capable of delivering this.

This exercise has to start by gaining as good an understanding as possible of what the organizational objectives are. Without going into the relative merits of the different project methodologies, even indicative budgets cannot sensibly be drawn up if it isn't known what the project needs to achieve. Nor can this be done if it isn't known, at least with reasonable confidence, what the technology solution is.

The cost difference between being able to using existing technology in which the project team has considerable expertise, and having to procure new technology with all the associated additional costs, is very great indeed. This could be the difference between achieving at least a 'minimum viable product', or nothing at all.

There must be clear evidence that the project objectives are reasonably understood and how these are going to be met - either with the existing technology, or what new solution needs to be procured. Otherwise, the project is likely to hit major problems. Evidence at this stage doesn't need to be documented to too great a level of detail but there does need to have been reasonably thorough discussions between business focussed and technology focussed staff on the project.

One sign that this hasn't been done properly would be if a new product has been chosen without detailed analysis of its functionality, with a mapping to that required by the project. If the product that has been chosen is one seen as 'sexy' and which it is likely that people are very keen to have on their cv, then that is even more concerning.

What to do about it ?

There are 2 main scenarios that have been covered – the management of new technology and of existing technology. They can be dealt with as follows –

• For a new technology, it depends at which stage the project has reached. It is important to try and make sure that as little time, money and effort as possible is wasted. If, for example, a new product has been purchased but neither staff training, nor supplier consultancy has been committed to, then the implementation should be put on hold until the suitability of the product has been properly assessed.

When the necessary ground work has been completed, then there is the decision on whether to proceed with the new technology or not. There will be much pressure to carry on regardless, but this would be to compound the error if the product really isn't suitable. However, even if this is the decision, at least the likely problems and costs will now be known.

• With the use of existing technology, at least no money has been spent. Unfortunately, sufficient time should have been spent on determining the suitability of the existing solutions as a platform for further development. It is important to gather a group (it will certainly require several people) which has an understanding of both the new functionality required, and a *realistic* view of the current estate. This is likely to require more than a single session, especially if it is identified that there is going to be a reliance on some of the less well known areas of the system.

If this requires something like a Feasibility Study (or whatever your preferred terminology is) to give reasonable confidence that you have a viable, affordable solution, then this is a very worthwhile investment for the project to make. (This is also an opportunity to document any poorly known areas of the estate.)

Put a tick in the 'Technology' box.

3. FASHION.

What is the issue ?

In many respects this is actually a subsection of 'Technology'. However, as it is a common problem with specific causes it deserves a section of its own.

The rate of development of new technology has been astonishing. Whether true or not, it has been said that if airplane technology had developed as fast as IT has, that Concorde would have taken off 2 weeks after the Wright brothers first flight. This was first said in the '90's. Even if it wasn't true then, it is probably true now. More importantly, it illustrates a rate of change, across a very wide range, that is impossible to keep up with. Even by focussing on a relatively narrow area, such as project management, it has become very difficult to maintain real expertise in all techniques and methodologies.

There are many consequences of this. It is inevitable that in an area this fast changing, that some of the new things that come along prove to be not as good as first thought. That is being polite of course. In reality, much new technology is very bad indeed but is hyped so that it achieves at least temporary 'success'.

Just selecting something new – be it a piece of technology or a new methodology, has become a major exercise due to the huge number of possible options.

Inevitably the in-depth analysis that would be needed is often just not possible. This can result in simply following the latest fashion (which is often created by whichever supplier can create the biggest hype rather than the best product).

There are at least 2 major potential consequences of just blindly following fashion. These are :-

• New technology is needed but the selection is made based almost wholly on what seems to be the most popular. As a result, sub-optimal technology is procured. It may be that there isn't anything wrong with the technology itself – it may actually work very well. It just isn't right for the specific organization or purpose it is being applied to. The consequences are :–

  o At best a mediocre solution, often implemented at much greater expense than was estimated. This results from the need to manipulate the technology to do something it isn't best suited for.
  o At worst, it could prove a complete disaster with everything having to be ripped out and the project started again – assuming the organization has the appetite to try again.

• The second scenario is when there is a decision to implement something because it seems to be what the competition is doing and people are afraid of missing out. So, a project is initiated to implement the latest fashion without any real understanding of what it is really about. This happens all too frequently. The history of IT is littered with terrible implementations of such things as Data Warehousing, CRM, Agile, Digital Transformation, Data Lakes – the list is depressingly extensive and covers just about every new thing that has come along in IT.

The consequences of this particular scenario often have long term impact. Not only is there the cost of the failed project but there is the probably greater impact of the loss of the benefits that would have been accrued. This is often made greater if the generic solution is seen to be at fault rather than the botched implementation of it.

For example, many organisations have not really understood what Digital Transformation actually is, and have simply re-built their current on-line systems. As a result, they have incurred cost for little or no real benefit. Worse, they now think the whole 'Digital' thing is just the latest hype, or an attempt by suppliers to sell them something. It could be years before they try again and reap the benefits.

There is another the danger if the technology was selected simply because it is the latest fashion. The staff who chose it may have no intention of staying beyond the initial implementation but rather be looking to move to a more lucrative role elsewhere.

Things to look for.

It is often difficult to differentiate between the

person who is genuinely trying to ensure that their organisation is staying modern and someone who just wants to have the latest thing on the cv or to play with some new technology. For either of the scenarios above, determining the reality will require some analysis. The first question is – why ?

If there is reason to suspect the situation is that of selecting a new product purely on its current popularity, then some of the questions to be asked are

- o Why are we selecting a *new* product ?
- o Do we *really* need something new ?
- o What are the problems with the current solution that are so serious that require its replacement?
- o If we do need a replacement how have we selected it ?
- o Was there a thorough Product Selection exercise ?
- o What real expertise in this area do we have which will have reduced the risk of making the wrong choice ?

If the answers are not very convincing then the chances are that this is just a fashion following exercise.

For the second scenario the situation is more complex because it is easy to get agreement that an organisation '*needs*' a CRM system, or *needs* to become Digital. However, if there is no real expertise in these things then only the smallest first step should be taken. The warning sign therefore is an agreement within the organisation that this new thing is needed without any evidence of the expertise that that decision is based on. The likelihood is that the organization has decided it needs something based mainly on the fact that other organizations have one.

What to do about it ?

For the scenario of making a selection by simply following the current technology fashion, the solution is relatively simple. Any decision should be very much evidence based i.e. the choice should follow a properly produced business case and product selection exercise.

If the scenario is that of choosing to implement a new type of business system e.g. a CRM system, more work is required. The most difficult problem is that it is likely that there is no real expertise already in the organization. Some people will probably still decide that it can be done without any additional help. While this self-confidence and enthusiasm can be helpful, this solo approach should be discouraged.

The next step should be about current staff, not just IT but all relevant areas of the organisation, learning as much as possible about this new thing. This should include a research phase to learn how it should be used and how others have done so successfully.

However, this second hand knowledge is rarely enough. Some form of real, practical experience is usually necessary to give the project the best chance of success. How you get that expertise is covered more fully in other sections but the key principle is to have help from people who are helping *you* do this rather than doing it *to* you.

Put a tick in the 'Fashion' box.

4. OUTSIDE the PROJECT.

What is the issue ?

This is a slightly different topic in that it is about things over which, by their nature, the project has no direct or substantial control. Arguably then, should this even be in this book ? The fact is – if there is something which will impact the project then it should be addressed even if there is comparatively little that the project *itself* can actually do about it. Examples are the following :-

Company re-organizations - apart from the distraction and consumption of management time, these have the potential to have an almost unlimited effect on the project. The impact could be anything from the loss of key personnel (especially at the Project Sponsor level), to a change of focus/scope, to outright cancellation.

Company take-over – this can have the same consequences as above or even greater. If your company is being taken over, then at the very least, it is likely that your project is put on hold while it is reviewed for conformance with a new strategy. Even if it is your company doing the taking-over the consequences can still be the same.

Change of strategy or policy – even if not driven by company changes of the type mentioned above, many companies will have periodic reviews of strategy to adjust for changes in circumstance e.g. economic conditions or political impacts.

Budget constraints – despite having a suitable project budget already agreed, changes in the over all company budget situation, or problems in other projects, can result in your project budget being affected. This is rarely for the better.

Resource constraints – as with budget, you may start off with sufficient resources, but things change. This could be anything from an expected hardware platform no longer being available to a loss of experienced staff.

Potentially with less impact, but still needing to be managed, is a change of project owner or sponsor. At the very least this is going to require management time bringing the new person up to speed on the project. It could also involve things like having to adjust to new ways of working to comply with the new sponsors preferred way of doing things, or even changes to the scope of the project.

Things to look for.

You don't need to look too hard to spot most of the things mentioned above. Being taken over by another company, for example, would be pretty hard to miss. (Sometimes a change of sponsor much less so.) Fortunately, as these are things which are outside the projects control there *shouldn't* be any blame attached to the project itself if they result in failure.

In the worst case, if it is proposed that the project be cancelled, this doesn't mean that the project should simply give up. Unless, because of the change of circumstances, the project no longer makes sense, then attempts should be made to overcome the problems. This is not least because a failed project is always going to look bad by association or on a cv.

What to do about it ?

While it isn't possible to do anything about your company merging with another, or indeed anything else on that scale (unless you just happen to be the major shareholder), what you can do is be as prepared as possible. Major organization change of whatever sort is (supposed to) be about improving the company. If your project does still deliver benefits within the new structure then logically it should be retained.

However, you should be prepared to find yourself in the situation of having to help 'sell' it again to a whole new bunch of people. While this should primarily be the job of the Sponsor, they may need help in the form of detail they don't ordinarily have, in response to questions they don't normally have to answer. Being prepared for this with suitable materials will also give the new decision makers confidence in the projects ability to deliver.

Indeed, for most forms of challenge to the project, having prepared a short, to the point, sub-set of the project benefit case would be very useful. While major organizational changes may be comparatively rare, issues such as budget challenges are, unfortunately, not.

Put a tick in the 'Outside' box.

5. TRUST.

What is the issue ?

As with any team activity, trust between the members of the project is vital for effective teamwork. On most projects real trust exists only within small groups – most often with people who have known each other previously or who work together a lot. There is then varying degrees of trust among the other members.

It is unrealistic to expect that people with any sort of normal life experience will walk onto a project, and from day one, trust everyone else on the project. That level of naivety would be quite worrying. What is essential is that a reasonable level of trust is achieved throughout the project because without it the project will not succeed.

Any project needs a disparate bunch of specialisms who rely upon each other to do their job well. The level of ultra-trust and interdependence demonstrated, for example, by the team that changes the tyres on a Formula 1 car, isn't what's needed. However, if at least a minimum level is not achieved then small groups will begin to make decisions for themselves. Soon, if it is not managed, there will be chaos.

If the trust needed doesn't develop it is likely to be for a number of reasons. Not least of these is that it is rare for any real effort to be made to build that trust.

While occasionally there will be 'team building' exercises which can have some benefit in the short term, too often this is merely a tick box exercise which most people will simply endure.

What is the nature of the trust that the project needs to have ? It is partly having belief in other people's ability to do their job to an acceptable level of competence, and partly a belief that others will support you to do yours (or at least not attempt to hinder you). Without this, project members will spend time distracted from their tasks, trying to identify what is 'really' going on, and attempting to protect themselves, or their group, from it. Or they could start duplicating tasks because they don't think that they will be done, or done properly, otherwise.

Things to look for.

The signs of this lack of sufficient trust are seen most clearly in the behaviours of the people on the project. It may be as relatively mild as a too intensive questioning of others progress and quality. However, it could be as relatively toxic as an insistence on the formal and extensive documentation of everything. At its worst people will spend too much time looking over their shoulder, checking what other people are up to. Progress will be slower than it should be and it will be of a start – stop fashion. It will also be a very unpleasant place to work.

What to do about it ?

The level of trust in a company is an integral part of the culture of that organization. As with so many other aspects, the culture of an organization comes from the top. The development of trust comes from things like - honesty in dealing with people, the acceptance of responsibility for mistakes, and not being too quick to simply blame other people for their mistakes.

Trust also develops from not tolerating the excesses of ego, from positives such as giving due praise for things well done and from demonstrating trust by giving people real responsibility. [The classic example of this is the way in which the Apollo 13 crisis was handled. Management trusted their really quite junior staff to find and implement a solution to the life and death problem with the spacecraft, and didn't attempt to micromanage the situation.]

A project team, on its own, will not be able to change the culture of the whole organization. It can however, create a microcosm of what is needed within their team. The level of trust that is needed does not develop overnight. But when people see real efforts being made to develop that trust through good example, and see how much it improves ways of working and the general tone of the workplace, then they will start to commit. The rest of the organization may even begin to join in.

Put a tick in the 'Trust' box.

EGO DRIVEN ISSUES.

This section is concerned with those *most* human of behaviours which badly affect the delivery of projects. To have the best chance of success, a project requires that many highly focused, ego-less, selfless individuals, put aside all their personal desires, needs and preferences, to focus exclusively on the delivery of the mutually agreed objectives. It doesn't seem very likely does it ?

Even worse, they are delivering something, 99.9% of which, is invisible to all but a small number of technical staff. One of the consequences of which is that it is very hard for most of those involved in an IT project to gauge actual progress. At least engineers, when building a bridge for example, can actually see how well it is progressing.

[This is one of the reasons why it is good practice to always take any opportunity to demonstrate the results of what you are doing e.g. producing a prototype ,and why working to a Minimum Viable Product is such a good idea.]

Why do some organizations more than others seem to have such trouble actually delivering projects ? One reason is because their corporate culture is all about the individual – personal ambition is what drives the success of their organization (if not their clients). This is the opposite of what is needed. The ideal culture is one of a mutually supportive team.

Alternately, some companies are too 'techie', they want all solutions to be perfect – with too little consideration of cost, timescales etc. The result can be the 'the operation was a success but the patient died' syndrome i.e. the technical solution was excellent but it didn't deliver the business benefits.

Despite the seemingly limitless choice of training courses, books and manuals which will tell us exactly what to do, for which type of project, when to do it, and how, people don't. Why ? The simple answer is - because we are human and therefore subject to a host of personal influences, prejudices, and failings such as greed, anger, selfishness etc. Obviously, these are a factor in almost everything covered in this book but they deserve analysing specifically in their own right.

If we ignore genuinely forgetting to do the things that the manual says should be done (which is indeed very human), then we can identify certain human frailties and wrongful behaviours which can actually cause, or certainly contribute to, project failure. Some of the components of what is meant by ego are as follows –

1. SUPERHERO.

What is the issue ?

Being a 'hero' doesn't *sound* like it should be a problem. By 'hero' is meant an individual who goes way beyond the normal contribution of any sort, to achieve the objectives of the project. Certainly our culture greatly admires heroes in their many different forms – be they the sporting or the caped variety. Where would the film industry be for a story-line without some hero saving the day ? Of course there are occasions when a hero is very useful to have. A particular technical expertise solving an intractable problem that had stumped others for example. Or an excellent piece of interpersonal skills in clarifying and agreeing a set of requirements from a complex and difficult group.

There is however a type of hero where the results are not so positive. In this scenario the individual is motivated not by the project objectives but by their own personal agenda i.e. self-promotion. Because their focus is not primarily on the needs of the project, all kinds of behaviours can occur. Such as –

- Creating fake alarms so as to be able to 'fix' them. Examples of this would include –

    - Raising false technical concerns that require a new activity to investigate. Which they, of course, resolve. Though only after a suitable escalation of concerns to senior people and the identifying of potential risks.

- Legal or 'political' issues which require bottoming out. As above, also requiring serious meetings with very senior people at which their strategic insight and exceptional analytical skills can be demonstrated.

- Taking on unnecessary, unproductive or even detrimental activities just to be able to complete them. This could take the form of –

  - Completely unnecessarily detailed documentation which doesn't stay current for very long and is quietly forgotten once the maintenance overhead kicks in.

  - Separate, but largely duplicate phases of testing, which can sometimes be necessary, but not for this particular project.

  - New, endless, over detailed, business process design work often at odds with the system being implemented and which therefore requires extensive customisation (and which quickly gets dropped when presented to the real world).

- Allowing things to go a bit wrong in order to create a 'fire-fighting' situation in which they can excel. This scenario is not uncommon in organisations with a highly competitive, 'can do' type culture. In this sort of organisation, doing things steadily, process driven, or by the book, doesn't get much attention or kudos. If there are no high profile fires to fight the danger for the individual is that an assumption is made by colleagues that, actually, their activity was probably a bit easy. Or it will be described as such as a means of down-playing their success.

So, it becomes necessary to create some drama. If the activity doesn't inherently have enough, then it must be created. This is a more subtle and difficult to manage scenario as the individual can't be seen to have mis-managed the activity in the first place or to be technically lacking in some way. A relatively minor, in reality non-concerning, delay could be engineered for example.

An area of the project would be chosen where the resource estimates are known to be on the high side. To get the activity back on track, huge efforts by the team are announced, requiring over-night or at weekends working. In reality, not too much new work is actually done as either the estimates were too high or less is actually delivered (e.g. see 'too much documentation' above). The main purpose is to get as much attention, from the most senior people, as possible. If this is managed correctly then the 'problem' is resolved and there is praise and congratulations for the individual. While close colleagues may well suspect what has actually happened, the wider project stakeholders will not.

These activities are high risk to the project. Even

the most cleverly managed, which don't result in actual project failure, still have a cost to the project in terms of the extra effort expended. There may also be software or hardware costs as well.

However, often the biggest impact is on the morale of the project. If the hero activity is regarded as being unnecessary (and it will be recognised as this by those closest to it), then it will be seen for what it is – a purely selfish and self-serving attempt to unfairly gain personal advancement. This is worse if it is also at the expense of a more deserving person or a better, more professional way of doing things. This creates antagonism and a poor team working environment which puts the whole project at risk of failure. Projects are a team sport after all.

Things to look for.

Without wishing to stereotype, it is often the personality type which is the first sign of this behaviour. It would be rare (though not impossible) for a shy, introverted
person to attempt this sort of activity. It is more likely to be the more extravert type who tends to be more risk taking and keen to get attention.

A hero needs events to react to, so if a project seems to be progressing comfortably and suddenly alarms are being raised about potential risks then suspicions should be raised. If those risks don't actually seem to be very likely to occur – they could in theory happen but the risk is vanishingly small, then this is likely to be an attempt to be a hero. If the 'problem' is fixed surprisingly quickly this is probably confirmation.

What to do about it ?

This behaviour is most likely, and best, spotted by close colleagues. It is particularly likely to be identified by those who may be about to be asked to work late nights and weekends to fix a non-problem.

Stopping this activity before it goes very far is obviously critical because if senior management has been convinced that there is a serious problem then much resource may be diverted to fix it. This could then cause real problems.

It is important therefore to discuss and analyse these issues as soon as they are raised. Embarrassing the 'hero' into dropping the issue could be counter-productive as they may otherwise be a productive member of the team. The issue must be investigated informally using other people who are close to it to get a balanced view. A likely conclusion to these investigations is a "humm, could be a problem, let's just keep a close eye on it for now and review again in a week. Thanks for raising this." Then quietly forgetting it.

Put a tick in the Superhero box.

2. DIFFERENT AGENDAS.

What is the issue ?

It is unfortunate, but true, that too often projects are managed based on a naïve, or at best simplistic, assumption – that everyone on the project agrees wholeheartedly on the objectives and how to achieve them. The reality is often very different. While most people will have a level of commitment to the project aims, these usually sit alongside their own personal objectives. If these are in a reasonable balance or at least not in conflict, then there shouldn't be a problem.

For example, it isn't a disadvantage to the project if an individual is keen to get experience of a specific technology on their cv. In fact, if the individual is motivated to work hard, learn as much as they can, and use that as input into what they produce for the project, then the project will almost certainly benefit.

However, if the desire to add to their cv is excessive, then the project will suffer. One example of this would be the introduction of an unnecessary or inappropriate technology. Not only is there the cost of the initial purchase of the technology, but then there are training costs, and the impact of poor productivity (at least initially). If the technology is inappropriate, or only marginally appropriate, then it may have, at best, no benefit for the project or it may even cause project failure.

Another example might be an over emphasis on

design techniques which become an end in themselves. In these cases excessive time and effort goes into, for example, the design of business processes to such a minute level of detail that they will never actually be implemented in practice. The individuals doing the design however get lots of experience to add to their cv.

However, differences in agendas can be even more malign. This can be as extreme as the individual who sees the project as being entirely about them. Their whole focus is on how they can gain personally from the project – be it financially, career or status wise. As long as the failure of the project does not affect them, then they don't really care what happens to it. At this extreme this could also include actively working to ensure that not only do they succeed but that others fail, or at least appear to. This could consist of anything from repeatedly pointing out even the most minor mistakes of others, to the 'saying yes, but doing no' scenario. At the very least this creates a negative and unproductive atmosphere.

Another extreme example would be an individual deliberately directing a colleague towards a tool or technique which they know will not work in that circumstance. When a problem occurs they will of course deny giving any such advice, or claim that they have been misheard or misunderstood.

One of the most destructive ways of attempting to ensure that others don't succeed is the use of selective, apparently objective 'reviews'. On the pretence of being helpful, these can be initiated on the work of others which is on its way to being successful. It is not difficult to find some grounds to initiate such reviews. For example, issues which are actually being successfully dealt with can be identified as requiring investigation. Governance groups are often not expert enough in the detail, and tend to be risk averse, that they can easily be persuaded to support the proposed review – if only because they fear being criticised later for not doing so.

The review is then managed in such a way as to cast doubt on the activity. This will be on some vague, evidence free basis, such as how it is being done or its likelihood of success. It is always possible to find something to criticize. Often it is the review itself which causes failure by disrupting the work of the staff involved. Even if this doesn't happen, the perception of the activity will often be tarnished to some degree and will at least reduce the credit that the individuals get for their work.

Things to look for.

Some of the signs of this 'Different Agendas' scenario are easy to detect, especially the more extreme examples. Initiating a review of a piece of work without very good reason, given the distraction this must cause, is very obvious. This is especially true if it appears to be just an individual or very small group who are proposing it.

Introducing new technologies when there has been no proper selection exercise or demonstration of real benefit is also easy to spot.

More difficult to identify is the case of excessive use of a particular technique such as in business process or technical design. These are often justified on the grounds of 'wanting to get it right'. However, a sure sign that these are being done to excess is when the activity is clearly dominating the time and resource of the project to a degree which just isn't proportionate. This could involve, for example, the production of huge quantities of documentation (which will never be maintained or even read in many cases).

What to do about it ?

If this behaviour is suspected, the emphasis must be put on the individual to justify what they are proposing. As mentioned earlier, sometimes the things that an individual wants to do are actually to the benefit of the project and should therefore be encouraged. However, the more extreme activities can only be justified if good cause can be demonstrated.

If there is any suspicion that, for example, a proposed review is malicious in nature and normal debate within the project team isn't enough to stop it, then this must be flagged up to the appropriate governance group. This should involve a discussion questioning the basis for the review and the bad impact it is likely to have on the project. It should also be made clear to the proposer that the team is aware of what they are doing.

All significant items must also go through a formal Change Management process.

Put a tick in the Different Agendas box.

3. PERSONAL PRIDE (based decisions).

What is the issue ?

This is the cause of so many problems. People decide that they know better than what the manual says they should do, or the company standards, or what their line manager says, so they do something different. This could be because they feel that their personal expertise or competence is being challenged. They feel resentment at being told to do something in a certain way when it is different to what they want to do. Or it could be because they are being told to do it by a line manager that they don't respect and they do something different simply to ignore or challenge their authority.

This is not a case of someone making an evidence based decision that their personal expertise is superior to the conventional wisdom or what the manual says. If done correctly, this can be a good thing, as no manual can possibly cover every possible circumstance and personal experience is a key element of all good decision making. This is different, this is the situation when someone thinks that to simply follow standard guidance or management direction somehow belittles them, so they do something different. No proper analysis has been done before they leap to a decision based mainly on their personal intuition or 'gut feel'. This is sometimes known simply as being contrary.

Things to look for.

The most obvious sign that this is happening is when people diverge from the standard way of doing things or from a recognized standard solution but with no evidence of any real reasoning behind the decision. If questioned, the justification is usually based on "I think….." or "I feel…." with no hard facts or clear evidence behind the decision. If their decision is blatantly the opposite of what it is known that their line manager would want them to do, then this is definitely a warning sign.

This type of behaviour can also occur from the more technical team members. This might take the form, for example, of a new or different product suddenly appearing, without ever having gone through any sort of formal selection process.

What to do about it ?

Picking up on this behaviour can either be done as part of more formal reviews by line managers or governance groups, or less formally by peers. Obviously this must be addressed and the decision corrected. Too often however a potentially difficult or embarrassing confrontation is avoided by the team. They just accept the bad decision on the grounds of deferring to the expertise of the individual – the "Well, if that's what you think , then I suppose it must be ok", approach.

Management should deal with it by an emphasis

on evidence based decision making rather than simply criticising the individual. This sends a message to the project team about how things should be done and avoids completely alienating an individual who may still have value for the project (especially if resource is in short supply).

It is often the case that the scenario is identified first by the individuals peers as they have the expertise to do so. Then it can be much more problematic. The culture of the organisation will determine to a large degree how this can be handled, as will the relationship of the individual to his peers. An open, friendly culture which supports an honest exchange of opinions means the situation can be dealt with fairly easily through discussion, without rancour. However, as this type of culture is often not the case, then the individuals peers must escalate it to line management. If, as is often the case, they are reluctant to do this, this is when Project Bingo comes into its own.

Put a tick in the Personal Pride box.

4. POOR TEAM WORKING.

There are so many different aspects to this, including -

a.   Personality Clashes.

Sometimes poor team work is simply down to what are often referred to as personality clashes - the fact that there are two apparently diametrically opposed personality types who just don't work well together. In theory this shouldn't actually be a problem as intelligent adults should be quite capable of ignoring minor irritations and work together in a professional manner. However, it is unreasonable to expect people to completely control their emotions over the often long period of a project. Naturally therefore, conflicts will occur and often surprisingly quickly in the pressured environment of a project.

a. Things to look for.

The most obvious sign is two individuals starting to argue over things that everyone else hadn't even noticed or thought important. These arguments also tend to be characterised by the individuals coming at the issue from such completely different angles that it can appear that they are actually arguing about different things. Often the argument will drag on long after everyone else's patience has run out.

a. What to do about it ?

You cannot change people's basic nature and

therefore address the fundamental cause of the conflict, (certainly not in the time available on the project!). It must be made clear to the individuals how irritating their behaviour is and attempt to keep them apart as much as possible. If this is done soon enough it can be done without upsetting them too much. However, to avoid these conflicts as much as possible it is also important to insist that discussions on issues are professionally based i.e. on evidence or facts rather than personal opinion. It is the responsibility of the individuals to provide that evidence.

Put a tick in the '**Poor Team**' box.

b.   Status Conflicts.

Unfortunately, too often, not working together effectively has more to do with status conflicts and competitiveness amongst staff. Rather than work efficiently on tasks, people will focus instead on assessing their personal position relative to others and hence who should be doing what. Or, if the relative status is clear but they don't like it, working out how to change the status quo i.e. get personal advancement.

One way of trying to get rid of an unwanted boss is to perform moderately, but 'by the book'. This would involve a person doing what has been asked of them but only half-heartedly or doing the absolute minimum required. Of course, this will not be done badly enough to actually be damaging to them. If their performance is queried the explanation given is that that was all they were asked to do. This deflects any blame coming their way onto their manager. The manager then gets the blame for the poor performance of the team.

b. Things to look for.

Deliberate non-co-operation can be well hidden. However, there are signs that can be picked up. Saying 'yes' but doing 'no' is the most obvious. People will appear to be working well, making team decisions, agreeing activities, making joint plans and even having fun together. However, all this apparent enthusiasm disappears once the team meeting is over and they go back to their desk and are no longer under observation.

The doing 'no' can simply consist of 'forgetting' to do the agreed activities. At its most extreme it can extend to actively implementing completely different decisions to those which were actually agreed. It isn't unusual for the failure to carry out the agreed activity not to emerge until the very last minute e.g. at, or just before, a progress or governance meeting. If the agreements had been carefully documented (and the pretence of good team working makes this less likely) then at this point there will be profuse apologies and claims of misunderstanding. However, the damage is done to the team lead because at the very least they have failed to manage properly.

Over all it will seem that people appear to be getting on well together, and working productively but that things are a bit of a muddle and there is a lack of clarity on what should be done. The result is that the team lead will be blamed for poor management.

b. What to do about it ?

It's been emphasised that projects are a team
sport and as such the human interactions need to be
carefully monitored and managed. Projects are not,
however, a social club. The obvious and crucial
difference being that the project team has been brought
together primarily to deliver a set of objectives. An
assumption that the apparent good team working is real
can be exploited by over-ambitious individuals. It is
important therefore that the formalities are observed
from the beginning – like documenting decisions and
ensuring that all individuals have signed up to them.
Back-tracking or divergence by individuals later will
therefore be clearly be identifiable as their fault.

Put a tick in the 'Poor Team' box.

5. 'DOG with a BONE'.

What is the issue ?

The title of this component refers to the habit of dogs, if they get a bone, to disappear into a quiet corner alone to chew on it rather than risk having to share it or have it taken from them.

As mentioned previously, personal agendas can be beneficial to the project if managed correctly but can be very detrimental if not. Another way that this can badly affect a project is when an individual is given the opportunity to step up and take on a significant responsibility. This could be for an specific phase, or as project manager, for example. The individual will obviously see the potential in this for their personal advancement. They can respond in very different ways. If they approach the task openly and positively, focussing on what will make the activity a success, managing colleagues and resources appropriately, then the project will benefit.

Too often however an individual will take a very different approach. Their focus will be on *them* – primarily on ensuring that everything to do with the activity is seen as to their credit. To some degree this is understandable. Particularly in highly competitive, unsupportive environments, such opportunities can be rare. It would be even more rare for an opportunity to come their way a second time if the first was not seen as particularly successful. Such chances have to be made the most of.

The unproductive behaviour tends to take the form of wanting to exclude as many others from involvement or ownership of the activity as possible (dog with a bone). This would include using as few other senior colleagues as possible, relying instead to too great a degree on junior staff. They do this because junior colleagues would not be seen as having contributed too much, and are easier to manage because they are not likely to dispute decisions.

In this scenario not only will the individual expect to get all the normal credit for success, but they will expect it to be even greater as they can point out that they achieved it with such junior resources. They are also likely to claim credit for their management skills in developing junior staff. Often these individuals will not even accept help or advice from their peers for fear of diluting the potential praise.

Unfortunately, there is much harm that can be inflicted on junior staff by this approach as they can be stretched too far, too soon. They are also unlikely to learn much of benefit from this type of manager, who has demonstrated by this approach that they are unlikely to be any good.

It is not uncommon for the individual to become exhausted by over extending themselves physically and mentally. If, as is likely, the activity is not completed successfully, the individual also has their career disappointments to deal with. In addition, they will feel resentment because they feel unfairly judged given the junior level of resource they had to work with ! However much they actually brought this upon themselves, they will not see it that way. So, amongst other problems there is now a disaffected member of the team and, very probably, unhappy junior members.

The result of this 'Dog with a bone' approach is that at best the activity will have been done less well than it could have been. More likely however, it will actually fail as the full potential of the organisation has not been properly exploited. Giving inexperienced staff more responsibility must be done with proper controls in place.

Things to look for.

There are a number of signs that this is happening. The most obvious is a very unbalanced (in terms of experience) team. It is rare for a manager to get all the resources they would ideally want, but a team which has big gaps in terms of levels of experience is a bad sign. If the individual given the opportunity seems content with this lack of experienced resources then this is likely to be a 'dog with a bone' situation.

Less easy to spot is when the task is for a single person and the individual is disappearing off in order to complete the task on their own. People are generally very busy on projects and a lot of management time can be taken up with fire-fighting activities. If something appears to not be a problem then there is a strong temptation to let them get on with it. As a result, the individual may receive little or no supervision or support.

What to do about it ?

In the unbalanced team scenario, because it is relatively easy to spot, it should be a case of trying to ensure a better balance in the team – even if the individual doesn't want the more experienced members. Refusing to take additional resource into the team if it is being offered would be so irrational as to be unjustifiable. If an individual did attempt to refuse the additional resource, then they will either need to be closely managed for the duration of the task or it is likely that it is they themselves who need to be replaced.

The case of the individual going solo is more difficult to spot. It wouldn't be unusual, for example, for them to cover up problems or lack of progress, by consistently reporting that all is well.

In both scenarios, more formally, visible deliveries on a regular basis are needed to ensure that the correct progress is being made. However, less formally, it is vital to ensure that no one is allowed to have exclusive knowledge of something. While an individual will be personally keen to gain the extra value that comes from having a scarce expertise, it is not good for the project or the organisation. Other staff must have access to this expertise through some form of 'pairing' or other knowledge transfer arrangement.

Put a tick in the Dog/bone box.

6. MASSIVELY RISK AVERSE.

What is the issue ?

Odd as it may seem, in some respects 'Risk Averse' is actually quite similar to 'Superhero'. These individuals are very, very keen to avoid any risk whatsoever - to the point of doing nothing if there is any perceived danger of failure. This involves identifying (though never quantifying), risks however small and creating disproportionate management activities to deal with them.

The similarity with the hero is that they both are guilty of identifying non-existent or trivial issues that urgently require major effort to fix. It is this misdirected and wasted effort that is a risk to the project.

The effort involved in these risk management activities will be massively disproportionate to the scale of actual risk or any potential consequences. In reality, the activity is often actually risk avoidance rather than risk management. Ironically, this type of behaviour is often seen, (as with 'superhero'), in very competitive, highly commercial, but unsupportive environments. Any real or perceived failure is catastrophic to an individual's career and therefore to be avoided at all costs. It does however have considerable cost to the organisation due to the resources wasted on the risk avoidance activity.

This behaviour is also found in environments with a low level of commercial activity. The difference is that in these environments, actual delivery of a project to timescales, cost and scope (or whatever the agreed objectives were) is not what is considered critical. Being seen not to appear to fail or not to cause any form of 'reputational damage' to the organisation or individual, is actually the critical thing.

It is important to clarify how the risk *aversion* described above is very different from risk *management*. Indeed, if the huge focus on identifying risks (i.e. things that could possibly go wrong), was accompanied by the proper management of those risks, then this would very likely be a benefit to the project. Instead, with risk aversion, risks tend to be either poorly, or not managed at all, because these individuals shy away from taking on this type of responsibility. In this culture, there is credit given just for identifying a risk without being expected to do anything about it.

Things to look for.

This type of behaviour can be relatively easy to spot. The most obvious is an apparent obsession with risk – it seems to be the only thing that these individuals talk about. However, the risk is only raised and left simply as – 'there is a risk that ....'. There is no follow up, the risk is not managed i.e. no analysis of the risk, no solutions are identified, resources are not allocated and the work to deal with it is not planned.

At best there will be the shirking of responsibility and an attempt to pass the problem onto someone else to deal with. As a result the project can grind to a halt because everyone agrees there is a risk, but no one will accept responsibility for it.

Another feature of this behaviour is the massive over estimating of the resources needed for tasks on the project. It may also involve identifying the need for highly specialist resource which, it is known, simply won't be available. This has the benefit to the individual of hugely reducing the chances of the task being late or over budget. Even better, the activity may be cancelled altogether because the cost is too high or is simply undoable due to a lack of the specialist expertise. This can be the best result for the individual as, often, they didn't actually want to do the activity for fear of failure. It means that if they do have to do it, they are far less likely to fail.

What to do about it ?

Similar to the 'superhero' scenario, the apparent 'risk' that much fuss is being made of, needs to be properly analysed. In particular, it needs to be assessed in terms of both the likelihood of it actually happening and what the real impact would be. Should an actual risk have been identified, with a significant potential impact, then it needs to be managed through formal Risk Management processes.

The risk aversion which results in significantly over estimating of the resources needed, is more difficult to deal with. If the risk averse individual is seen as the expert in an area it will be hard to argue with the estimates they have come up with. The solution is to identify a similar activity, perhaps on another project, and discover the actual resources that were needed. No two projects are ever exactly the same, but a roughly comparable, real project, with actual figures is going to be more persuasive than the guess of a so called expert.

Put a tick in the 'Risk Averse' box.

7. SELF DELUDED – don't know what they don't know.

What is the issue ?

It is a pretty old truism that those that know the least and are the least experienced are often the most confident in their knowledge. Conversely, the greatest experts frequently appear unsure of themselves. This syndrome is *very* prevalent in IT. It's cause is obvious. It is only after years of accumulating knowledge, and experiencing the many, many things that can go wrong in a very complex environment, that you realize how little you actually know and have still to learn.

There are different variants on this scenario but the one discussed here is when the individual doesn't know what they need to know, but doesn't realize it. This most commonly occurs when the individual simply doesn't have the experience to recognise their lack of knowledge and their excessive enthusiasm causes them to blunder on. Given the complexity of most IT systems today, with their increasing levels of old or out of date software, and high level of interdependence, this can have major consequences.

Things to look for.

If the people involved are known, then there are some very obvious indicators - such as the fact that the individuals don't have very much, or perhaps even any, experience in the thing they are about to take on. They may not even have had any training but might still be about to launch into something.

It could be even worse if the composition of the whole team looks very junior, with no obvious, more experienced, individuals in it. If this team is from a supplier brought in to enhance existing resources, then the chances are that this project is the training ground for this team. This may be great for them but it is unlikely to be for the project.

It may be that the thing to be undertaken is very new - a recently developed piece of technology for example or a very different methodology. In this case not only can the enthusiastic individual not possibly have any expertise but not very many other people will have either. Getting real help will therefore be difficult. Any problems will also be compounded if the technology turns out to be less than perfect (i.e. always).

What to do about it ?

If a colleague is about to embark on something which is more than just a simple task and which you know they have no expertise in, then they should be stopped. However keen or enthusiastic they may be – that simply isn't enough. Proper training and/or some form of mentoring is essential. No one wants to destroy anyone's enthusiasm, but it needs to be properly channelled in a professional way.

Fortunately, in this scenario the individuals

enthusiasm will usually deflate fairly quickly if they are challenged. Most often they will accept, when it is pointed out to them, that they don't really have the experience needed.

The difficulty tends to come with mounting that challenge unless there is already someone in the organisation with the relevant, specific experience. If not, then finding an example of someone else's experience and what was required (from the supplier perhaps) will be necessary. If that isn't possible, pointing out, in purely generic terms the missing expertise (e.g. "you have 0 months hands-on experience") will have to suffice.

Related to this, with respect to new technology, there is general rule about not implementing software with a '0' at the end - especially if the number in front of the 0 is a '1'. If the software is that new then no one has any experience in it and it must be treated with great caution.

Put a tick in the Self-Deluded box.

8. KNOWINGLY IGNORANT.

What is the issue ?

It has been said that it will be written on the gravestone of humankind, 'They wouldn't learn their lessons'. By this is meant that we keep repeating the same mistakes, that we don't learn from history (which, in a way, is what this book is about). This section is similar to the last but differs in that it is about the scenario where individuals press ahead regardless of the fact that they don't really know what they are doing – but know they don't !

Again, as previously, this kind of behaviour can, in the right circumstances, be not only very valuable, but even crucial. A scientific researcher for example knows that, in a sense, they are ignorant of what they are doing. Explorers of all kinds are the same. If people didn't persevere anyway, despite their known ignorance, we would all still be living caves or whatever humans lived in originally.

The point about these examples is that there is no alternative. The whole point of the activity is to add to the sum of human knowledge, things which are currently unknown. Most importantly, they are approached using a methodology which allows the activity to be properly managed. The project activity I'm referring to is different because there *are* known ways of doing these things. Unfortunately, the individual or team choose to proceed even though they haven't learnt it.

Any individual could make this mistake if they have the right combination of laziness and ambition but probably the most common example of this is the 'consultant syndrome'. (This refers to a generic behaviour pattern rather than a specific group of people.) The scenario is that of an individual or team in a situation where they want to, or feel obliged to, or perhaps are even being forced to, undertake an activity that they have little or no actual expertise in.

This situation often occurs when external consultants have demonstrated huge expertise in something in order to win some business. Unfortunately, the people who actually turn up to do the work are a different set of people entirely – and have no such expertise. This is sometimes referred to as the 'A' team vs the 'B' team approach. This is when the A team win the business but it is the B team (or C or D) who actually arrive to do the work.

Also, people on a short term contract will often make dubious claims to specific expertise and hope to survive long enough to actually learn enough about what they are doing. If recruiting anyone has been difficult they may have months before being ejected. This is known as the 'fake it 'til you make it' approach. If no one else knows anything this often works.

The problem with this situation is that, at best, the project is likely to be late and over budget because estimates were not originally developed on the basis of using very inexperienced staff. In the worst case the project is cancelled because of soaring costs or because it emerges, when enough experience has been gained, that the wrong technology has been chosen. Still, some people might get to put new, cool stuff on their cv.

Things to look for.

This is very similar to the previous section but with added difficulty - especially if the people involved are not well known e.g. they are external. If this is the case, their real level of expertise can be hard to determine. The obvious indicators would be that the individual or team cannot clearly demonstrate much experience in the area they are about to take on. This is different and more difficult from the last scenario because the individuals involved, if challenged, are likely to push back and insist that they _do_ have the necessary expertise. They will 'big up' every single piece of experience that they have, however slight. Given the lack of internal expertise, it can be very difficult to mount that challenge as the right questions and answers aren't known.

What to do about it ?

The approach to this is largely determined by whether the people involved are internal or external staff.

If internal staff, then their determination to press ahead with something despite their lack of qualifications is relatively easy to identify and deal with. This can be made into a positive thing by using that determination but insisting on them receiving the right training, support etc. and ensuring that the project budget and timescales reflect this reality.

If external staff, their determination is most likely being driven by commercial and personal advancement considerations. Assessing their actual level of expertise is difficult. So, once whatever references etc. as are available have been properly followed up, it is a case of carefully controlling the work. This should be broken down into very short phases of activity so as to be able to closely monitor what is happening. Progress to the next stage should only be on the basis of the successful completion of the previous one.

Put a tick in the 'Known Ignorance' box.

9. MAKING ASSUMPTIONS.

What is the issue ?

We all make assumptions. Nothing much would get done if we checked out every single thing before doing anything. However, in this section it is the larger scale assumptions that cause projects to fail that we are concerned with. These would include such things as products selected or methodology chosen. "Assumption is the mother of all cock-ups" is a saying which crystallises this issue. We proceed on the basis of something being correct, when we don't actually know if this is true. Inevitably this can have dire consequences.

Assumptions are made for a number of reasons, such as :-

- Laziness – we can't be bothered to do the research. We know there is ground work to be done investigating options but, actually, we can't be bothered to do it. It is easier just to plough on without doing the hard, often uninteresting, work.

- Ignorance – we don't realize that there are other options to investigate so blindly just carry on with what we think we know.

- Time – we know there are other options but don't explore them because we think we don't have the time to do it. This may or not be the case (see 'Laziness').

- Money – we don't think the budget will run to exploring the different options so we proceed with just the one we prefer and hope it is right.

In order to explore this scenario it is useful to think of assumptions as being of two types – Known Assumptions and Unknown Assumptions. 'Laziness' and 'Time' are examples of Known Assumptions. 'Ignorance' is an example of an Unknown Assumptions.

Of the two, Unknown Assumptions are by far the most dangerous, as all kinds of unexpected catastrophes could result. With the Known Assumptions, alternatives may have been proposed, but been quickly dismissed. In this case there is at least the knowledge, if only at the back of people's minds, that what is being done may not be right. People will at least be more likely to be alert to signs of things starting to go wrong.

Things to look for.

The type of behaviour that is typically displayed when people are relying on assumptions is a lack of analysis in their thinking. With known assumptions, even if alternatives were proposed, there will have been a much too superficial discussion on these. Concerns about the amount of work required and the time it is likely to take will have shortened any debate and any alternatives proposed will have been dismissed with little or no justification.

With unknown assumptions, there will not even have been a brief debate. Instead of pausing to consider options people just charge ahead with whatever is the most obvious thing. It is clear that the main consideration is time and getting the thing done. This will be most obvious in the situation where, for example, different technical products or methodologies are available but not enough time is taken to consider which is the most appropriate choice.

What to do about it ?

Some assumptions must be made or we end up with the 'paralysis through analysis' syndrome. However, what is needed is the judgement to know when to assume and when not. Achieving this judgement is usually based partly on experience (often from previous mistakes) but also from having a mindset which is aware of the danger of making assumptions and automatically looks to consider options. In most cases asking the initial questions, "Is this right ? Are there other, better, options?", requires only a short discussion and can be answered relatively quickly.

If these can't be answered quickly then this is often a warning sign and it is likely that time taken to really consider options will be well spent. If this saves even one mis-step on the project then it will have been worth the effort.

Put a tick in the Assumptions box

10. POWER.

There are many potential aspects to this. The two that are most relevant and so are covered here are – 'Power Corrupts' and 'Power and Responsibility'.

10a Power Corrupts.

What is the issue ?

There is a reasonably well known quotation, "Power tends to corrupt and absolute power corrupts absolutely." (Lord Acton). The amount of power given to any individual on a project is too little to corrupt anyone very much, but it can distort their behaviour. People can find themselves in a position of power and attention on a project the like of which they have never had before – either in work or outside it. This could be the result of –

- Having large numbers of staff when they are not used to it.
- A budget much greater than people at their level in other parts of the organization would normally have.
- There are also potential suppliers, eager for business, suddenly being their new best friend and ego booster.
- There is the attention that is suddenly given within the organization. It is really the project that people are interested in, but they will often flatter the project team to get their preferred item of scope included or they may want some insider information.

It isn't a surprise therefore if it goes to people's heads to some degree and results in poor decision making.

Things to look for.

The adverse effect of power doesn't necessarily show itself in raging dictatorial or maniacal behaviour – though it can do. Rather, it is often a quiet (even smug), over confidence. The result can be a lack of discussion or consultation on key decisions with those who may actually have greater expertise in specific areas. This refusal to consult is especially likely if these experts are seen as too junior.

There is also a tendency to make overly quick, even abrupt decisions because they think consultation would be seen as weakness in someone in their lofty position. Sometimes decisions are even made just to demonstrate that they have the power to do so.

What to do about it ?

A key question is - is the decision making power in the right places in the project ? For example, is the organization overly hierarchical ? Or is the power positioned where the expertise is? Flatter structures, with empowered individuals able to make decisions based on their expertise, is a much more successful way of making correct decisions on projects at the speed that is necessary. However, it does require that decision making power is devolved to more junior staff.

Few, especially the more traditional managers, are comfortable with devolving power. In some circumstances they are right. For example, no project exists in a political vacuum. Like it or not, the politics have to be managed and this requires individuals who have skills and experience in this area. What is needed is clear areas of responsibility where staff have the authority to make decisions within their expertise.

However, while the 'delivery' personnel on a project need to be given the space and empowerment to get on with their job, they must also have a clear escalation route to individuals who can manage cross-project issues such as politics. These individuals need to behave like ice breaker ships – clearing a route so that those following can do so at maximum possible velocity.

Put a tick in the Power box.

10b Power and Responsibility.

What is the issue ?

Too often people find themselves in the situation of having either power without responsibility, or the opposite, which is responsibility without power. For most, the usual experience is finding themselves in the latter situation. Both are bad of course.

The former is often the result of a bad management structure. For example, if someone has the power to insist on a particular technology without having to take responsibility if it proves to be wrong. The consequence is bad decisions being made and implemented, not least because there are no repercussions on the individual making the decisions. These individuals tend to be happy in their job.

The latter, responsibility without power, can result in good decisions but which never get implemented because the person does not have the power to do so. These individuals tend to be very frustrated.

In both cases the project will suffer.

Things to look for.

People making decisions for which they are not going to be held responsible will tend to do so quickly and without going through any sort of formal process. Why bother after all, with a tedious process, if they have the power to ignore it and won't suffer any consequences ? Worse still is if it is an area in which they actually have very little expertise. This might seem unlikely but it does happen in organizations where promotion isn't entirely on objective competence and as a result people get promoted into positions where they have no expertise.

It also happens where there is a belief that managers should be generalists. It is not unusual for the individual to like the power they have been given and be reluctant to give it up. So, they tend to exercise the power quickly before anyone has the chance to try and debate their decisions.

It won't be difficult to spot the latter situation as people with responsibility without power will quickly let their frustrations with the situation become as widely known as possible. They will complain about their sense of helplessness and their inability to get things done. This will of course have a bad effect on the morale of the project, not least because others will fear being put in the same situation.

Unfortunately, they will very rarely complain to the people who might actually be able to do something about it - because of the culture of the organization which created this situation in the first place.

It is important to identify these problems quickly as the impact on staff morale will happen before the impact on project progress and is therefore a sort of early warning signal.

What to do about it ?

By having too hierarchical a structure, power is concentrated into a small number of people who may have gotten to that position in any number of inappropriate ways. Crucially, to do these super-roles well requires a combination of experience, intelligence , wisdom, interpersonal skills, political nous etc. which in practice is far too rare for every project to have the number of these people that they would need.

Projects need to organize accordingly, with

delivery teams self-managed as far as possible. Other individuals with specific specialist or 'softer' skills (e.g. political, interpersonal, financial, negotiating etc.) should be located where they can be called upon to aid the project when needed. While there still needs to be a decision point at which this all comes together if agreement cannot be reached, the structure under this individual (or small decision making group) should be much flatter than is too often the case.

Put a tick in the Power box.

11. CONSPIRACY of SILENCE – keeping problems hidden.

What is the issue ?

Why, when people involved in a project know that things are not going well, and that the actual status is being very over optimistically reported, do they not call it out ? People will sit in executive meetings where the status of a project is supposed to be being discussed and major problems don't even get mentioned. Many people are guilty of presenting things in as good a light as possible at times (while working furiously to get them back on track). This is of a different order. Everyone in the room is aware, perhaps to varying degrees, that there are serious problems, but no one is mentioning them. What is going on ?

One possible answer is that *everyone* has something they would rather not have discussed. They sit, watching the clock, desperate for the meeting to be over as soon as possible. They are hoping that nothing will be said that forces them to reveal their own particular problem. As a result, they don't mention the problems that they may know that other people have, because they know that that would free the other people to mention theirs. It ends up a conspiracy of silence driven by a fear of a sort of mutually assured destruction (MAD !).

There are other possible causes of this conspiracy of silence. Some organizations have a culture of not raising issues which could cause embarrassment. It is considered to be 'not the done thing' to embarrass a colleague in a meeting by raising difficult issues. This behaviour is maintained because people who join committees very quickly sense what the unwritten rules are and follow them in order to fit in. This is especially true if they have been recently promoted or are new to the organization.

People also avoid mentioning their particular issue if no one else has mentioned theirs because no one wants to be the only person with a problem. They think – "I'll wait until someone else mentions their problem first - then mine won't stand out so much." The result is that it doesn't get raised, and more importantly, dealt with.

Another common reason for problems not being discussed openly is the fear of a more senior manager. Even if peoples responsibilities are going well and they are not worried about a discussion on issues, they *are* afraid of a more senior individual who they know *does* have a problem. So, this issue doesn't get discussed and as a result is less likely to be fixed.

These scenarios can easily mean that serious problems simply don't get raised. Often, even if an issue is mentioned, for example it is listed on the Risk Register and therefore must be covered as part of the agenda, it is dismissed briefly as 'just about done'. The rest of the committee go along with it, - with supportive murmurs and nodding of heads .

Things to look for.

This scenario is easy to spot on any steering committee or other governance group. There will be unrealistically little, or even no, discussion of issues, a certain discomfort in the atmosphere can be detected, and people will be keen to move on as quickly as possible.

For those not on any such committees then the signs are less obvious and more difficult to detect on large projects. Most people will only have real visibility of their own, relatively small part of the project. It will only become more widely obvious to people that there is a problem in another area if a dependency hasn't been produced and there is an impact on their area. At this point the problem has usually become much harder to fix - if it is even fixable by that stage.

What to do about it ?

The fundamental problem is often the culture of the organization. Amongst the worst is one which is dominated by different types of fear. This includes fear of confrontation of any sort, or fear of the management hierarchy, or an excessive fear of failure.

It doesn't even have to be as extreme as fear. In very hierarchical organizations it is common for there to be a culture of great deference. This has almost the same effect. People simply do not attempt to question what is being done – not least because they know that more senior staff would, at best, simply ignore them.

The culture in an organization takes time to change and must be driven from the highest level. This will not happen in time to save the project. Approaching senior management is unlikely therefore be the solution.

At the project level, a possible answer is to ensure that the situation doesn't arise in the first place. This could be done by creating a sort of 'mini' culture within the project. For example, it is one of the fundamental purposes of a daily 'stand up' to create an atmosphere in which everyone can, indeed must, be honest about what is really happening. This works, because everyone knows, from the beginning, what actually *is* happening! By creating this atmosphere from the beginning it is more likely to last throughout the project. This approach also has the benefit of not relying on management to identify and fix problems but rather puts the onus on the team members.

As a key element in team building, the 'stand up' is one of the mechanisms by which project members can ask for, and receive, help and support for their problems. As a result, problems don't fester or become compounded but are dealt with as early as possible. It is important also in creating a 'no blame' culture which allows individuals to make mistakes without being overly criticized and for the team to help solve the problem.

The solution is more difficult if the problem is occurring at the Steering Committee or governance level. Unfortunately, it is also at this level that the problem is most likely to occur. This is because the members will have little by way of team spirit due to not often working closely together. These meetings may well be a rare exception to that.

To avoid needing a brave (or suicidal) individual who is prepared to ask the difficult question or to confess their own problems, one solution is to *really* use the project plan. Simply walking through the plan, particularly focusing on the inter-dependencies, is often enough for previously unreported problems to be forced to emerge. It is one thing to cover up a problem but quite another to blatantly lie about progress against a plan when asked.

This process can be facilitated if a relatively small problem is identified first and brought into the open. This has the effect of warning people how things are going to work and that other, more serious, issues are also likely to come to the surface. They will realize that they need to either fix their problems themselves, or find ways to bring them up for resolution by the wider group in a way that will not be damaging to them.

Put a tick in the "Conspiracy of silence" box.

IN ESSENCE

There are 28 different scenarios or situations which are described in this book. Some occur more commonly on projects than others and some are very definitely more damaging to a project than others. However, they all, to some degree, are the cause of projects to fail to deliver what was promised. There are also others which may be added at a later date.

It is not the intention of this book to provide a scientific analysis of which of these occur most frequently and the degree of damage that each can do. Rather it is to make the reader aware, or perhaps just to remind them, that these behaviours exist and to help develop a mindset which is on the lookout for them and so be alert to the dangers.

As each project is very specific to its own circumstances with, as a result, the degree of the scenarios varying, an accurate general analysis would be impossible, but more importantly, valueless.

If the reader has read through this book in a relatively short space of time it may be that they find the overall impression very depressing. This would not be surprising as the behaviours described are not humans at their best. However, it is not the intention to put people off working on projects, quite the opposite in fact. By recognising and accepting that humans can be selfish, inconsiderate etc. the purpose is to help avoid the worst consequences of these behaviours and so make projects more enjoyable to work on.

Given that humans behave as they do, and are unlikely to change any time soon, and that currently the result is the very high failure rate of projects, the question must be asked – why continue to do them ? Surely what we have is an example of the triumph of hope over experience ? Why not accept reality and just stop and try something else ?

This actually refers to something mentioned earlier in the book – there is a view that no good software has ever been developed by a team of more than 3 people. In this scenario there is no need for a project as we know it, with a methodology to drive it or an organisation to support it !

Attractive as this might sound (except to project managers perhaps), unfortunately the days when business systems of the complexity and sophistication required today could be built by 3 people are long gone. What can be learned from those 3 person developments is the vital importance of such things as good communication, trust and teamwork (and having a manageable Tea club).

If there is a single most important point to make about project failure it is that projects are actually just **too damn hard to get right** to be able to do anything other than focus relentlessly on what the right thing is for the project. Any deviation from this for reasons of ego or politics or personal agendas inevitably dooms the project to failure. The best advice has to be – focus on doing the right things but keep an eye on the politics – and manage the people well.

PROJECT BINGO.

Why Project Bingo ?

Spotting that there is a problem on a project is relatively easy – or at least some are, by some people. However, it is very difficult for any one individual to see all the problems on a project and even more difficult to do something about them. Not least of the difficulties is that no one is expert enough in all areas to know if something is going wrong.

What is needed is to bring as many people's expertise to bear as possible. On an ideal project there would be perfect honesty and trust and people would not be too shy to speak frankly about what they think is a problem. Such projects are unfortunately too rare.

In the absence of this perfect world, what is needed is threefold –

- Something which helps identify problems, with some suggestions on how to fix them.

- A means of raising these issues within the project team on a normal project. If the culture is such that people are afraid, or even just too shy, to raise issues, then much expertise and valuable feedback will be wasted.

- The issues on a project which are likely to cause a failure, must also become visible to the wider project governance. Otherwise, there is a danger that they will be kept hidden by the very management which is failing to deal with them properly.

The first of these is addressed by the main body of this book. The purpose of Project Bingo is to address the other two by providing a way for all staff to draw attention to things which they believe are an issue. This needs to be done in such a way that stakeholders, or anyone who has an interest, can see what the **project team** thinks the state of the project **actually** is.

This might seem a distraction, or worse, a cause of endless debates on the right thing to do. Given the wide range of roles and hence perspectives on even a medium sized project, there will be plenty of diversity of opinion to fuel these debates.

However, while playing this game would require considerable openness (and self-confidence) by management, on well managed projects it will be at the very least a valuable additional source of knowledge. On badly managed projects it will provide much needed and important feedback to the wider project governance on real risks to the project.

It will also be a potentially vital release valve for staff to vent frustrations which may have no other outlet.

How to play.

There are a total of 28 separate sections in the main body of the book. Each of these should have an entry on the bingo 'card'. The card should be copied and printed (or drawn on a convenient whiteboard) and put somewhere where all staff have access to it. Ideally this would be somewhere where people could add to it without being seen e.g. the kitchen or other communal area. Staff add to it by putting a tick in whichever boxes they think apply to their project.

There is no reason to limit the number of ticks that each member of the team can add. It is unlikely however that any project will have ticks in all 28 boxes. (If it did, the project would be in such a bad state that it wouldn't need Project Bingo to point out the problems.)

No doubt some people will abuse this (there is always one) and add many, many ticks in a box that particularly concerns them. This isn't a problem as Project Bingo isn't intended to be an exact analysis of the project. In addition, it at least emphasises what someone thinks is a very serious issue and this is much better than that issue not being raised at all.

A sample Project Bingo card is shown in the appendix.

APPENDIX

A typical bingo card would look something like this : -

PROJECT NAME :

SCOPE CREEP		POLITICS	ASSUMPT			BAD TEAM
	RESRCS		FASHION	SELF DELUDE	DOG & BONE
IGNORANT		BUS. CASE		WRONG TECH.	
POOR DECISION	POWER	SILENCE	OUTSIDE		PLANS
	SUPER HERO	BAD ORG.		POOR TEAM	
ESTIMATE			MORALE		RISK AVERSE
	MGT QUALITY			DIFF AGENDA	
TRUST		FEAR	PERSON PRIDE		BAD COMMS

Printed in Great Britain
by Amazon